Questioning Assumptions

Rethinking the Philosophy of Religion

Tom Christenson

Fortress Press
Minneapolis

QUESTIONING ASSUMPTIONS
Rethinking the Philosophy of Religion

Copyright © 2011 Fortress Press. All rights reserved. Except for brief quotations in critical articles or reviews, no part of this book may be reproduced in any manner without prior written permission from the publisher. Visit http://www.augsburgfortress.org/copyrights/contact.asp or write to Permissions, Augsburg Fortress, Box 1209, Minneapolis, MN 55440.

Cover design: Joe Vaughan
Book design: PerfecType, Nashville, TN

Library of Congress Cataloging-in-Publication Data
Christenson, Tom.
 Questioning assumptions : rethinking the philosophy of religion / Tom Christenson.
   p. cm.
 Includes bibliographical references (p. 135).
 ISBN 978-0-8006-9753-2 (alk. paper)
 1. Religion—Philosophy—Textbooks. I. Title.
 BL51.C534 2011
 210—dc22
                                  2010033211

The paper used in this publication meets the minimum requirements of American National Standard for Information Sciences—Permanence of Paper for Printed Library Materials, ANSI Z329.48-1984.

Manufactured in the U.S.A.

15 14 13 12 11 1 2 3 4 5 6 7 8 9 10

CONTENTS

Preface	xi
Introduction: Focusing the Question	1
The Recurring Debate: Does God Exist?	1
God versus Science: The Dawkins/Collins Debate	5
Does God Exist? Was There a Time when the Question Did Not Arise?	7
Mythos and *Logos*	10
Questioning the Questions	12
From the Classroom: Student Questions and Responses	13
Questions for Reflection	14

Part One: Questioning the Philosophy of Religion

Chapter 1: Questioning Assumptions about Religious Belief	19
Assumption 1: Believing Is the Focal Act of Faith	19
A. Not All Religions Are Belief-Focused	19
B. Even Religions That See to Be Belief-Focused May Not Be as Much as They Seem	21
C. Assuming That Faith Is Belief-Focused Narrows Our Vision	22
D. Believing Is Not an Intentional Activity	25

  E. Believing Is Too Cognitive and Too Logo-Centric to Be
    the Focal Act of Faith   26
  F. Many Serious Thinkers Have Suggested Other Things
    as Being Religiously Focal   27
  G. The Term *Believe* Is Not Univocal   32
  From the Classroom: Student Questions and Responses   39
  Questions for Critical Reflection   42

Chapter 2: Questioning Assumptions about God's Existence   45
  Assumption 2: The Basic Religious Question Is about the
    Existence of God   45
  A. God Is Not a Thing That May or May Not Exist   45
  B. Does God Exist? Being Fooled by a Misdirected Question   46
  C. Does God Exist? Being Fooled by Grammar   48
  D. Does *X* Exist? The Temptation of the Question   50
  From the Classroom: Student Questions and Responses   51
  Questions for Critical Reflection   53

Chapter 3: Questioning Assumptions about Religious Language   55
  Assumption 3: Religious Language Is Primarily Referential   55
  A. Referential and Nonreferential Meaning   55
  B. My Son's Atheism   57
  C. How Is God-Language Used?   57
  From the Classroom: Student Questions and Responses   61
  Questions for Critical Reflection   63

Part Two: Rethinking the Philosophy of Religion

Chapter 4: Rethinking Religious Faith   67
 Religion as a Way of Seeing   67
 Religious Language as Parable?   73
 Poetry: A Prerequisite for Faith?   74
 Faith and Imagination   76
 Religious Faith: An Imagination-Shaped Way of Seeing   76
 Some Prejudices against Imagination   77
 The Power of Imagination: Some Testimonials   81
 Religious Imagination   82

Religious Faith as Experiencing-As	84
A Critical View and a Response	85
A Theory of Religious Discourse	89
From the Classroom: Student Questions and Responses	92
Questions for Critical Reflection	94

Chapter 5: Rethinking the Rationality of Faith — 95

The Question of the Rationality of Faith	95
Newton's Scientific Achievement Revisited	96
The Democratic Achievement Revisited	97
The Pragmatic Examination of Religion: James, Nietzsche, Marx, and Freud	100
Some Problems with the Pragmatic Critique	107
Preliminary Conclusions	108
Fruitfulness as a Criterion?	109
Faith and the Fulfillment of the Human	113
Is Religious Faith Rational? One More Time Around	117
Some Concluding Thoughts	121
Some Implications	122
From the Classroom: Student Questions and Responses	124
Questions for Critical Reflection	126

Glossary — 127

Works Cited — 131

Annotated Suggestions for Further Reading — 135

Index — 139

DEDICATION

I wish to dedicate this book to the students who have, over the decades, enlivened the philosophy of religion courses I have offered. They have kept me both awake and honest. Their questions and challenges inspire my continued learning. I believe a teacher is a communicative learner. I hope my students have learned something of value from me, because I certainly have from them.

PREFACE

A couple of decades ago, I was privileged to hear a talk and reading by Gary Snyder—poet, nature writer, and one of the West Coast group who hung out with Jack Kerouac, Lawrence Ferlinghetti, and Allen Ginsberg. They later became known as the "Dharma Bums" and "the Beats." After Snyder's reading and talk, a student asked him, "We know that you are a long-time student of Buddhism, so tell me, how has your religiousness influenced the way you write poetry?" Snyder was silent for a moment and then replied, "I'm not religious; I'm a Buddhist." Needless to say, the student was disappointed. His question had not been answered. What Snyder had done instead was to question the assumption built into the question. Might the student have learned more from having his question questioned than from having his question answered?

I tell this story because I expect that a similar sort of disappointment may very well descend on many readers of this book. I suppose there are many who might ask, "Do you believe in God or not?" and "Whether you do or not, what are your reasons for doing so?" and "If you do not believe in God, what alternative cosmological theory do you have?" If those are your questions, I'm going to disappoint you, because I'm not going to answer them. Instead, I'm going to challenge them and question the assumptions they make.

It is extremely important to see that even our opening questions make assumptions and that these assumptions are often what most need to be questioned. But that is exactly what philosophy is—the uncovering and questioning of really basic assumptions. As my friend and former colleague Sig Rauspern frequently says, "To start with the right question is to have done half the inquiry."

Universities and colleges across the country offer courses in the philosophy of religion. These courses may differ from one another in some particulars, but they also share many things in common. Almost all of them, I venture to say, are focused on the question of the rationality of religious belief. And that question is focused, in turn, on the evaluation of theistic arguments, that is, arguments about the existence of God. When people put together texts or anthologies for such courses, they keep this focus well in mind. Louis Pojman, in the introduction to his much-used text *Philosophy of Religion*, articulates this common focus very clearly:

> What is the truth about religion? We want to know if religion, or any particular one at least, is true. We want to assess the evidence and arguments for and against the claims in an impartial, judicious, open-minded manner. This I will endeavor to do in this book.
>
> The key notion of most religions is the idea of God, an all-powerful, benevolent, and providential being, who created the universe and all therein. Questions connected with the existence of God may be the most important we can ask and attempt to answer. If God exists, then it is of the utmost importance that we come to know that fact. (5)

I cite Pojman's introduction here neither because I find fault with it nor because I want to recommend it over others but simply because I think he has aptly articulated the typical focus of the philosophy of religion. This focus is the reason why any good anthology in the philosophy of religion will include the classical arguments for God's existence as well as the critiques of those arguments and will include discussions of the problem of evil and discussions about the reasonableness of theistic belief.

For decades I have taught an annual class on philosophy of religion. Like most such classes and most textbooks prepared for such classes, it begins with the question of the rationality of theistic belief and with an examination of the classical arguments, pro and con, regarding the existence of God. We employ texts (like Pojman's) and anthologies designed for such courses. But over the years, my students and I have discovered that this way of beginning makes a host of significant assumptions, including:

- that belief is the focal and most important part of religious faith
- that the most important belief is theistic belief—that is, belief that God exists—because this is the belief that religious people are assumed to have that atheists and other nonreligious persons lack
- that religious language is primarily referential and that it refers to a being, God, whose existence/nonexistence is the crucial question (The knowledge of God's existence, if it is possible, is the knowing of "fact," as Pojman puts it.)
- that existence is the proper mode of reality for thinking about God.

As students of philosophy, it is part of our task to articulate and examine these assumptions once they become apparent to us. The critical examination of these assumptions is how I have shaped the second half of my class on the philosophy of religion. The first half of the class does philosophy of religion the way it is customarily done. It is essentially a generic course in the philosophy of religion. The second half deconstructs the first; it critically examines the assumptions on which the first part rests. How would we have to rethink the philosophy of religion if we discovered that many of the assumptions of its most common arguments are questionable?

This text is a guide to this process of thought. It attempts to make the assumptions of the typical philosophy of religion course explicit and to question them. It then considers some alternative ways of thinking about these matters. Knowing that the text would be used for the second half of a philosophy of religion course, I have tried to keep it reasonably short but without its inquiry being merely suggestive. This text could also be used to introduce a more advanced study in the philosophy of religion. For example, I have a friend who has used an early draft as a text for his students in a seminary course.

The text has four main sections. The first focuses on the oddity of the "Does God exist?" question, which tends to focus much of philosophy of religion as it is usually taught and studied. The second section explicates and challenges three assumptions that philosophy of religion makes. The third section suggests an alternative view of the nature of religious language and religious faith. The fourth section shows what the consequences of this alternative view would be for the understanding of the question "Is religious faith rational?" Since the argument of the text is fairly complex, I have tried to make the structure explicit, following a topical outline format where I think it will help student readers.

Although each section is unique, they all also share a common structure. Each pursues an inquiry and makes an argument and often includes a discussion of the work of some particular thinkers for purposes of contrast and illustration. Each chapter contains a set of questions posed by students (From the Classroom: Student Questions and Responses) in a philosophy of religion class where a draft of this text was used. The students asked such helpful and probing questions that I decided to include the questions and my responses to them at the end of each section. In some cases, the student questions indicate a misunderstanding or misreading of the text. But that too is helpful since I then get an opportunity to correct misunderstandings others are also likely to have. At the end of each chapter, I also include questions for discussion—*Questions for Critical Reflection*—that may serve as prompts for students who are eager to pursue these issues more deeply.

Introduction: Focusing the Question

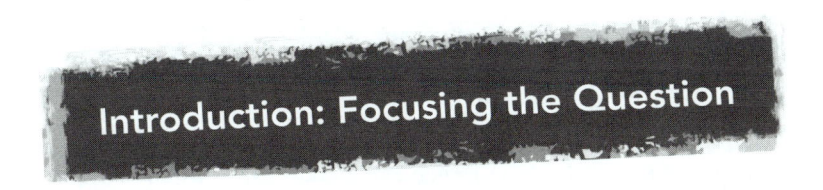

The primary question of the philosophy of religion has been, "Is religious faith rational?" That question has usually been translated into a second question: "Are there good reasons to think that God exists?" Most philosophy of religion texts (and courses) focus their attention there, examining and evaluating the reasons pro and con for the existence of God. But it is important to notice that the first question leads to the second one only if we are willing to make various assumptions—about what religious faith is and what role theistic belief plays in it, about how religious language works, about how God is related to human life and experience, about whether "existence" is the correct way to talk about the reality of God, and so forth.

In this text, I wish to challenge all of those assumptions and consider some alternative ways of looking at faith, religious language, and the reality of God. Eventually, we will reexamine the question about the rationality of religious faith. But here, at the outset, we will begin with the question about the existence of God.

The Recurring Debate: Does God Exist?

Your studies up to this point will probably have acquainted you with a variety of theistic arguments, that is, arguments for or against the existence of God. These arguments have taken three basic forms over the centuries.

Cosmological arguments are arguments from the existence of the cosmos to its cause. Generally, such arguments take the following form: all events have causes; the universe (or its beginning) is an event; therefore, the universe must have a cause. The cause of the universe cannot be an event in the universe, so it must be a supernatural cause sufficient to create the universe. Such a cause cannot itself have a cause. It must be the uncaused cause, and this must be God. There are variations on this argument. Thomas Aquinas generated three different versions on his own, all found in his *Summa contra Gentiles* (1264), which has influenced Christian thought on this topic ever since its publication.

Critics have noted that the argument seems to both assert and make an exception to its first premise. If every event has a cause, then what was the cause of God? Isn't it a bit odd that every event needs a causal explanation except God? Why make an exception in one case and not in another? If we're going to allow God to be self-caused, then why not allow the universe to be self-caused? A second line of criticism argues that causal language makes perfectly good sense when applied to events *in* the universe. We can meaningfully ask "What caused the Grand Canyon?" or even "What caused the solar system?" But when we apply the idea of causality to the entire universe, do we any longer understand the concept or the question or any answer we might give to it? Have we gone beyond the meaningful employment of the concept of cause?

Ontological arguments take the following form. Let us assume that anyone who understands the word *God* understands that it refers to an ultimately perfect being, a being who lacks no perfection. But any being who did not actually exist could not really be ultimately perfect, for we could then easily imagine a being that was more perfect, namely, one that actually existed. So, an ultimately perfect being must exist; otherwise, it would not be ultimately perfect, and that would be a self-contradiction. Two famous statements present this argument, one by Anselm of Canterbury in his *Proslogion* (1077) and the other by René Descartes in his *Meditations on First Philosophy* (1641).

The most effective criticism against this argument was brought by Immanuel Kant in his *Critique of Pure Reason* (1781). Kant argued that the ontological argument makes the assumption that existence is a perfection, that is, a quality that a most perfect being would not be lacking. Kant points out that existence is not a quality but a prerequisite of having actual qualities. We do not, when describing a thing, delineate all its qualities and then add, "Oh yes, and it also has the quality of existing." Existence, Kant maintains, is not a quality; hence, it is a mistake to think of it as a perfection. Consequently, it is a linguistic and logical mistake to argue that it is a perfection that a most perfect being would have.

The third general type of theistic argument is the *teleological argument,* or *argument from design.* There are more arguments of this type, and they vary widely. One by William Paley in his *Natural Theology* (1802) runs as follows:

Particular parts of the universe (as well as the universe itself) are extremely complex, intricate, and well adjusted to one another. The human eye, for example, is an amazing organ. Its design is exceptionally well adjusted to its function, at least as well adjusted as the design of a watch is to its function. The solar system itself operates according to physical laws that also bring to mind the intricate adjustment of parts found in a fine watch. If we were to find a watch while walking in the woods, we would naturally suppose that it had been made by a fine watchmaker and that it had been designed for the purposes to which it seems so finely suited. So it is also quite reasonable to suppose when we find intricate works and adjustments in nature that they have been designed and created with such purposes in mind. Such a designer and creator is, of course, a wise and powerful God.

There are many critical responses to this form of argument. First, there are parts of the universe that seem well designed and well adjusted, but there are also parts that seem chaotic and ill adjusted. Why is the human body, for instance, sometimes allergic to its own disease-fighting antibodies? Does that show careful design and workmanship? It's quite amazing that fish lay eggs and reproduce their kind, but is it also a sign of careful and wise design that only one in one thousand of these fish eggs survives into adulthood in order to reproduce itself? Second, we've seen watches being made and repaired, so when we find a watch, we very legitimately conclude that this new one has also been designed and made in the same way. But we've never seen a universe being made, so the analogy that the inference depends on is weakened by this important difference.

Third, as in the criticism of the cosmological argument discussed earlier, one may here also ask, "Do we understand what the terms '*creator*' and '*designer*' mean when applied at the level of the universe?" Probably the most effective criticisms of the design argument come from the work of David Hume and can be found in his book *Dialogues on Natural Religion* (1779). Finally, a more recent criticism came to light after the publication of Darwin's *On the Origin of Species* (1859). There, we are led to consider an alternative explanation of the adjustment of purpose and design of something like an eyeball. If the design of the eye did not serve well the life of the organism that possessed it, then that species would have died out. Thus, it should be no surprise that organisms that survive have eyes and other sense organs well suited to the lives they lead. Evolution, rather than a wise designer, provides an alternative explanation.

Arguments concerning the problem of evil are also generally included among theistic arguments. Although they take a variety of specific forms, they generally argue as follows. Assuming, as the ontological argument did, that God is a perfect being, then God would have the characteristics of being all powerful, all knowing, and completely beneficent, that is, willing only what is good for the creation. But if God has these characteristics, then why is there evil in the world? Given the perfection of God, evil is a problem.

There are a variety of responses to this problem. First, what seems like evil is always seen to be so from a limited point of view. The rabbit regards the presence of a fox family as evil, but from a larger, more ecological view, it is part of a larger design. The tidal wave that kills thousands of people seems evil to those affected but is actually a necessary part of the "best of all possible worlds." Responses of this sort are usually called *theodicies*. One of the more famous of these arguments can be found in the work of the German mathematician and philosopher Gottfried Leibniz (1646–1716). We might like to think that the world would be a better place without certain features (poverty, disease, natural disasters), but the removal of such features would result in a worse world overall.

A second response to the existence of human evil has generated what is frequently called "the free-will defense." God could have made us morally perfect creatures, who would never do the horrible things we do to one another. But God could not have done so without taking our free will away from us. So we are allowed to pursue our own life choices (including evil ones) in order that free will may be preserved. One of the most famous of these arguments is by Alvin Plantinga in his *God and Other Minds* (1967).

All of these arguments can be, and usually are, examined in greater depth in any philosophy of religion text or course. Here, however, it is our purpose simply to be reminded of what they are and how they talk about God, God's existence, and God's relation to the world and human experience.

As shown by the dates noted in connection with these arguments and their criticisms, this dispute has been going on for a very long time. If we were to peruse contemporary philosophical journals, we would discover that they are still going on. There are contemporary philosophers who attempt to revive each of these three forms of argument and at least an equal number who sharpen new criticisms to be brought against them.

God versus Science: The Dawkins/Collins Debate

The November 3, 2008, edition of *Time* featured as its cover story "God vs. Science." The accompanying articles included a debate between two scientists: Richard Dawkins, noted biologist, author of *The God Delusion*, who is one of the foremost anti-religious polemicists, and Francis Collins, also a biologist, director of the National Human Genome Institute, and a convert to Christianity. Here is a small slice of their conversation:

Time: [Question directed to Dr. Collins.] Both of your books suggest that if the universal constants, the six or more characteristics of our universe, had varied at all, it would have made life impossible. Dr. Collins, can you provide an example?

Collins: The gravitational constant, if it were off by one part in a hundred million million, then the expansion of the universe after the Big Bang would not have occurred in the fashion that was necessary for life to occur. When you look at that evidence it is very difficult to adopt the view that this was just chance. But if you are willing to consider the possibility of a designer, this becomes a rather plausible explanation for what is otherwise an exceedingly improbable event—namely, our existence.

Dawkins: People who believe in God conclude that there must have been a divine knob-twiddler who twiddled the knobs of these half-dozen constants to get them right. The problem is what this says, because something is vastly improbable we need a God to explain it. But that God himself would be even more improbable. Physicists have come up with other explanations. One is to say that these six constants are not free to vary. Some unified theory will eventually show that they are as locked in as the diameter and circumference of a circle. . . . The other way is the multiverse. That says that maybe the universe we are in is only one of a very large number of universes . . . as the number of universes climbs the odds mount that a tiny minority of universes will have the right fine-tuning.

Collins: . . . I actually find the argument of the existence of God who did the planning more compelling than the bubbling of all these multiverses. . . .

Dawkins: . . . What I can't understand is why you invoke improbability and yet you will not admit that you are shooting yourself in the foot by positing something just as improbable, magicking into existence the word God.

Collins: My God is not improbable to me. He has no need of a creation story for himself or to be fine-tuned by something else. God is the answer to all of these "How it must have come to be" questions.

Dawkins: I think that is the mother and father of all cop-outs. [pp. 5–6, online edition]

We should notice several things about this discussion. First, the debate is about the best explanation for the existence and state of the universe. It is about which, of the two views considered, is the best theory. That is the implication of the banner headline, "God vs. Science," as though these were rival answers to the same question, that question being, "What is the best explanation for the cosmos?" Collins maintains that God is that explanation, whereas Dawkins argues that the universe will ultimately explain itself and that no mention of God is necessary in such an account.

Second, the God whom they disagree about is a being, the grand creator and designer of the universe. The type of argument Collins is advancing is what has classically been called a design argument. The universe, he argues, shows evidence of careful design. Therefore, there must be a designer, and this designer everyone supposes to be God. If the narrator were to say, "It seems to me that both of you actually believe the same thing, namely that you neither know nor understand the ultimate cause of the universe? You simply disagree about what that great unknown should be called; one of you calls it God, the other calls it science," I'm sure both Collins and Dawkins would strongly object.

Third, the debate focuses on probability and improbability, though it frequently seems that Dawkins and Collins are not using these terms in exactly the same way. To ask about the probability of God is to ask something oddly different from asking the probability of a particular event or state of affairs. Or, do both of them believe that creation is or was an event? One thinks such an event happened, whereas the other does not? Neither seems to be bothered by talking about gauging the probability of this cosmos, or about gauging the probability of God. Both, it seems to me, have taken the language of probability far beyond the point where we understand the questions or the answers.

Fourth, although both are famous biologists, neither seems able or even likely to change the other's mind. That makes one wonder whether their beliefs are based on their reasons or whether their reasoning is based on their beliefs. Another explanation might be that they are like two trains rushing toward each other but on different tracks. Just when we expect that they will crash, they pass by without actually encountering the other, and both emerge, ideologically, without a scratch.

Finally, some interesting questions could arise in such a discussion. Perhaps they did, and the *Time* editors left them out. In any case, their exclusion is itself significant. Is the language of physics sufficient for describing the whole of reality? Is theistic language necessary and appropriate in order to give a scientific (i.e., causal) account of cosmogony? I would answer no to both of these questions. Is this what a discussion about the rationality of religious faith should be about? Once again, I'd answer no. The fact that these questions are not even raised shows much about the assumptions with which both Dawkins and Collins are working. When two disputants share common assumptions, it can be fruitful to articulate those assumptions and question them. Yet, there are assumptions here that neither seems willing to recognize or to question.

"Does God Exist?" Was There a Time when the Question Did Not Arise?

If we read through the extant documents of ancient and classical civilizations, we will find a great deal of religious literature. The poetry of the ancient Greeks, for example, is full of references to the gods and their interactions with one another and with humans. Hymns, myths, architecture, and sculpture are dedicated to, or depict, these gods. But in spite of all these references, there is little questioning about whether these divine beings exist.

It seems to have occurred to no one in the Hellenic world to climb Mount Olympus to see if the Olympian gods really resided there or to check out whether Persephone made her annual spring trip back to be with her mother, Demeter, and her annual autumn trip back to the domain of her husband, underground in the realm of the dead. Perhaps these myths were told and heard with a strand of irony that made the hearers understand how they should and should not be taken. We hear that Socrates was accused of atheism, but his accusers seem to have confused atheism with simply not believing in the right gods, the gods of the Athenian community. No critical reader can take such a charge seriously. Besides, the accompanying charge was that Socrates was inventing new gods, so it hardly sounds like atheism in the sense in which we use the term today.

Why, in this early age of first science and philosophy, was there so little discussion about the existence of the gods? The only piece in the ancient literature that looks like an argument for the existence of the gods was offered by stand-up comic and philosopher Diogenes the Cynic (412–323 BCE). He remarked that there must be gods, for how else could one explain the stupid behavior of one of his contemporaries, Lysis, whose wits seemed to have been blasted by them.

One major exception to the general silence on the topic is the philosophy of Aristotle (384–322 BCE). Aristotle constructed an argument in his *Metaphysics:* an account of the universe is not complete without a nonredundant account of its cause. The ultimate cause of the cosmos cannot be a never-ending series of causes because then the question is not answered, only indefinitely postponed. There must be, therefore, a self-caused cause of everything else. This must itself be a continuing process that lacks nothing. Aristotle concludes that this must be God thinking about God's own perfect nature. The perfection of God is thus the ultimate final cause of all other processes in the universe. It's interesting to note that Aristotle does not identify this divine process with any particular god of the Hellenic world or of any other religion. Nor does Aristotle conclude that any particular worship of this God is appropriate. In some ways, the activities of every organism and mechanism in the cosmos are motivated or inspired by the perfection of this uncaused cause.

In the Hebrew Scriptures, God is heard, obeyed and disobeyed, praised, accused, questioned, lamented, challenged, and addressed in prayer and hymn. But God's existence, at least, does not seem to come up as an issue. Why wasn't this a pressing question or the focus of lively debate? Why is it not a question that focuses attention in the Greek and Hebrew Scriptures or the Christian Gospels, the Epistles of Paul, or the Qur'an?

Was it because these people of time past were too pious or too obedient or too uncritical or too stupid to doubt the existence of the divinities they worshiped? I don't think so. Certainly, among the writers of the ancient world are some of the most critical, reflective, and inventive minds in human history.

Why, then, weren't they questioning the existence of God or the gods? Let me suggest two explanations.

First, God or the gods were the focus of worship, not objects of thought. *Which* god or gods one worshiped was an interesting and viable question, a question of some concern and interest, but it occurred to almost no one to question whether there were even gods to be worshiped. Imagine a conversation with a friend about what each of you values most highly. An interesting discussion might well follow. But imagine a third person walking in and questioning whether there *is anything* to value, that is, whether values exist. The question strikes us as wrongheaded. The very fact that we value things is all the evidence one could want that there are such values. The question "Yes, but do values exist?" seems weird beyond belief. I think the question "Do the gods exist?" was weird in exactly this way to ancient peoples and people of the classical past.

Nicholas Lash (2004) explains it this way:

> For most of our history, then, 'gods' were what people worshiped. I do not mean that people worshiped things called 'gods'; I mean that the word 'god' simply signified whatever it is that someone worships. In other words, the word 'god' worked rather like the way 'treasure' still does. . . . there is no class of objects known as 'treasures'. There is no going into a supermarket and asking for six bananas, a loaf of bread, two packets of soap and three treasures. Valuing is a *relationship*. Treasures are what we value.
>
> . . . There is no class of objects known as 'gods.' Worshiping is a *relationship*; gods are what we worship. [10]

Worshiping, in other words, helps establish the meaning of the idea of God. It proceeds that way rather than first establishing whether God or the gods exist and then deciding whether or not to worship this God. We begin to understand what God-language means by noticing what worship is.

This brings us to the second possible explanation of why the question about the existence of God or the gods did not arise in those earlier times. Religious language (prayers, hymns, sacred stories, dramatic enactments) was understood in its life-orienting role rather than as a set of assertions about some supernatural realities. The implication of this explanation is that religious language was assumed to be not primarily descriptive or fact assertive but life orienting. We read about Moses' encounter on Mt. Sinai not primarily to tell us something about Mt. Sinai or about Moses but to tell us something about the life and worship focus of this covenant community. In a parallel way, my saying "I love you" to my beloved is not a *description* of how I feel nor about how much love is contained in my love glands (glandular secretions can, after all, be measured) but is about my intention for the orientation of my life in the present and the future. It *looks* grammatically like a description, but it *works* much more like a promise. In asking, "Do you love me?" the beloved is looking for a commitment, not for a description. So the grammar of some religious language may look descriptive, but it functions as a language of orientation and commitment.

Before it can occur to people to begin questioning the existence of God or the gods, both of these explanations must change. God or the gods must come to be thought of as beings, asserted by the believer and denied by the unbeliever, whose existence may be questioned and defended. The existence of God was not a pressing issue in the ancient or classical world because people had not fallen into thinking this way. But it is the way many people (lots of philosophers among them) think today. We commonly assume that *faith* equals *believing* and that the primary belief is belief in the existence of some entity called God. If one begins with such assumptions, then, quite naturally, the next question will be whether there is such an entity. If one does not make these assumptions, on the other hand, the question will seem oddly wrongheaded and unnecessary.

It is the thesis of this book that accepting these assumptions and adopting this way of thinking was not an advance but a very deep conceptual mistake, a mistake about language and a mistake about the nature of faith. If I am right about that, it is a mistake that has had dire consequences for both philosophy and religion. It continues to confuse many people, both religious and nonreligious.

Mythos and *Logos*

For a very long time, historians of thought have treated myth as though it were a kind of pre-rational theory. Before people learned how to offer theories based on evidence and reason, the common account ran, they offered myths. We, living in a postmythological age, see the inadequacy of myth as a theoretical explanation and therefore see philosophy and science as necessary and more successful attempts at the same thing. We read myth as though it were primitive theory, and we evaluate it on theoretical grounds. Myth is thus dismissed as weakly supported theory. That seems to be what Dawkins's dismissal of religion is based on. But what if myth is not, and never was, an attempt at theory? What if it is something quite different, functioning in a different way in the lives of humans? To fault myth for not being very good theory is like faulting a dancer for not being a very good football player. The appropriate response is not to defend against such charges but to point out, "Dance is not poorly executed football; it's not football at all. Something completely different is going on there."

Myth is more than a story about some past event or state of affairs. Myth is simultaneously about the past (grammatically) and about the present and the future (intentionally). It is essentially connected to ritual and to the complexities of human life. Myth is a life-orienting telling and doing. C. Stephen Evans, in his 1996 book *Why Believe?*, comments that "religious beliefs are not primarily intellectual *theories*, about which we can easily suspend judgment. *Religious convictions concern life and how it should be lived*" (8). And Karen Armstrong, in her best-selling book *The Case for God* (2009), writes:

> Myth and ritual were [from the beginnings of human culture] inseparable, so much so that it is often a matter of scholarly debate which came first: the mythical story or the rites attached to it. Without ritual, myths made no sense and would remain as opaque as a musical score, which is impenetrable to most of us until interpreted instrumentally.
>
> Religion, therefore, was not primarily something that people thought but something they did. Its truth was acquired by practical action. [xii]

As a consequence of this, the adequacy of a religion cannot be evaluated by an armchair theorist who regards its documents as so many theoretical propositions. It can be adequately judged only by one who has participated in the myth, ritual, and the life form that it shapes. To anyone else, it will seem incredible and fantastic. And it will be quite misunderstood. Religion is a practical endeavor, life shaping and life changing. That's why it has to be so much more than believing the right dogma or assenting to the right propositional belief.

Armstrong goes on to trace both the source and the consequence of this misunderstanding. She writes:

> The rationalized interpretation of religion has resulted in two distinctively modern phenomena: fundamentalism and atheism. . . . Atheism is parasitically dependent on the form of theism it wishes to eliminate and becomes its reverse mirror image. . . .
>
> I am concerned that many people are confused about the nature of religious truth, a perplexity exacerbated by the contentious nature of so much religious discussion at the moment. My aim . . . is simply to bring something fresh to the table. [xvi, xvii]

That is also one of the purposes of this book.

That the question of the existence of God or the gods seldom arose in ancient civilizations is not all by itself a reason we should not raise the question.

There are also several other reasons, many of which are presented in the sections that follow. Together, I believe they make a strong case.

Questioning the Questions

Many people (including most thinkers who argue about the existence of God) suppose that religious faith and the God-language it generates addresses such questions as "What caused the universe?" and "What happens to us after we die?" Such a beginning rests on the assumption that religion will answer for us questions that are at the edges, beyond our experience and our normal powers of knowing.

I would suggest instead, echoing the twentieth-century Christian thinkers Dietrich Bonhoeffer and Thomas Merton, that religion answers questions that are at the very center, questions such as "What does it mean to be human?" and "How are we in the world?" and "How are we with others?" The first set of questions sees God as transcendently high, transcendently long ago, or transcendently into the future. The second set see, God as transcendently deep and, odd as this may sound, transcendently present. The former questions are, I think, ones that can be avoided, or at least we can avoid answering them by simply saying that we do not know enough to answer them. The latter questions are ones that all humans answer in one way or another by the way we live our lives.

If the role of philosophy of religion is to evaluate how well religious faith responds to its foundational questions, then getting those questions right is crucial. We will return to this issue in chapter 5, which asks, "Is religious faith rational?" Should it be a fair evaluation of religious faith to discover that it does not produce a convincing cosmology or an evidence-responsive biology? I would say, "No." Is it, on the other hand, fair to critique religious faith because it does not provide an adequate or workable life focus? I would say it is.

It is extremely important to see that even our opening questions make assumptions and that these assumptions are often what most need to be questioned. But that is exactly what philosophy is—the uncovering and questioning of really basic assumptions.

FROM THE CLASSROOM: STUDENT QUESTIONS & RESPONSES

Q: When I first encountered Anselm's version of the ontological argument, I was very confused by it. But now I think it makes very good sense. I paraphrase it this way: "A God that doesn't exist is no God at all."

R: That's a very provocative way of putting it. But I don't think it works very well as an argument. Suppose we imagined a wonderful cure for cancer; it's readily available, it does not require surgery or other invasive therapies, and it doesn't seem to have any negative side effects. How happy we'd all be to hear news of such a thing. Then someone asks, "It sounds wonderful, but is there such a thing?" At that point you respond, "It must exist, because a cancer cure that doesn't exist is no cure at all." We may agree with that sentiment, but I doubt we'd be convinced on those grounds that such a cure is actually available.

Q: Dawkins and Collins seem to be arguing about whether God is a good and necessary scientific theory. Why won't Dawkins allow God as simply an alternative scientific answer? Scientists, after all, seem willing to consider more than one theory.

R: If you're interested in Dawkins's view, I suggest reading him in more detail. He has a lot to say about this issue. But for now, let me just suggest this line of argument: if something is going to count as a viable theory in science, then it has to meet the criteria of a good scientific theory; it has to be based on evidence, it has to be verifiable or falsifiable, and so forth. Dawkins doesn't think that God meets those criteria.

Q: Isn't it likely that people didn't question the existence of gods because they were afraid to? Socrates was, after all, put to death even if the charges were not coherent.

R: I'm sure that was true of many people in the ancient world, just as it may be true of some people today. But, curiously, Socrates was willing to do other things that ended up getting him in trouble. Yet, he seems to take at least some of the Hellenic divinities very seriously. I don't think he was doing that because he was afraid of the authorities. I think he didn't question their existence because it was not an issue that particularly interested him or made sense to him.

Q: Is it Armstrong's point that both theism and atheism are a mistake? Does that make her an agnostic?

R: No. I believe she would say that all three of these alternatives are modern phenomena and part of what she calls "the rationalized interpretation of religion." Theists believe that God exists, atheists believe that God does not exist, and agnostics think that there are not sufficient reasons to draw either conclusion. All three positions assume, however, that "Does God exist?" is the right question. Armstrong wants to challenge that assumption, and, as you'll find in the next chapter, I do as well.

QUESTIONS FOR REFLECTION

1. Are there other kinds of arguments for the existence of God than the three types mentioned?

2. Is the Dawkins/Collins debate typical of contemporary arguments about religion? Do you know of others who approach the issue differently?

3. Can you think of alternative explanations for the relative lack of attention given to the issue of the existence of God or gods in the ancient world?

4. What difference does it make to discover that myth and ritual are inextricably linked? How does that change our reading of myth? How does it change our participation in ritual?

5. Armstrong's music analogy suggests that myth is to be "read" like a musical score is read—as a set of instructions for performance rather than as a source of information about another world. Can you think of significant differences between reading music and reading a myth? What worlds are each related to and how?

6. The quotes from Evans and Armstrong support the idea that we do not need to establish the existence of God before worship makes sense. In fact, we may learn the meaning of God-language only in the midst of worship and the life it helps shape. Can you think of other situations where that is the case—that is, where we learn the meaning of an idea by participating in a form of life?

Part One

Questioning the Philosophy of Religion

1. Questioning Assumptions about Religious Belief

Assumption 1. Believing Is the Focal Act of Faith

If you ask a group of college students for a definition of religion, nine out of ten will say, "Religion is belief in a divine being (or beings)," or something very like that. Such comments mirror the culture in general because this is the way most people think about religion. Why do most people think this way? Because this is what most people think. That may sound like a stupid thing to say, but it does reflect a real situation. We pick up our ways of thinking from the culture, and the culture is us. It is, to borrow a term from the computer world, the default setting of our minds. The fact that most people think this way is not, of course, a good *reason* for our thinking this way, but it is a relevant *cause* of our doing so.

We should realize how deeply ingrained this assumption is, in others as well as in ourselves. We should not suppose that it will be easy to change people's minds about this very common and deep-seated belief. For reasonable people, such beliefs are changed only when they have good reasons to think otherwise. So, what kind of reasons can be given for questioning the assumption that *believing is the focal act of faith*? Something is religiously focal if it is both essential and primary. What follows are seven reasons for questioning that assumption.

A. Not All Religions Are Belief-Focused

When the term *religion* is mentioned to an audience of Americans and Europeans, we are likely to think about it in terms of what we know about Christianity since it is the dominant religion in most parts of Europe and the Americas. Consequently, it is easy for us to infer that "since Christianity is belief focused, other religions are as well; it's just that they have different beliefs." I can remember making that assumption myself when, several decades ago, I spent some time in a Native American community (Yankton Dakota) in South Dakota. I was interested in their religious practices and ceremonies and got to know the tribal spiritual leader well. One day, I asked him, "Tell me about your religious beliefs." He smiled at me silently and shook his head. Finally, he said, "You have seen us dance, you have heard us drum and sing, you have heard our stories and prayers, you have eaten our sacred meal, you have even joined us in the sweat lodge, and you have shared in smoking the pipe." I replied, "Yes, and I thank you for allowing me to do all these things. But now I want to know about your beliefs." This time, he laughed out loud and said something in his native language that his friends also laughed at. "What does that mean?" I asked him. "You are suffering from white man's mind," he said. "We should do a healing ceremony for you."

He refused to talk about any beliefs. At the time, I was tempted to take this as a sign of his lack of theological sophistication, thinking, "He doesn't know the beliefs." It only later occurred to me to think, "He doesn't tell me the Dakota beliefs because there aren't any." Given more experience in Native American communities, I would now say that though there may be some beliefs, they are not an important part of the Dakota religion. If there are beliefs, they are not focal. In fact, to focus on beliefs, as I did, is an improper approach to the Dakota religion. The proper approach is singing, dancing, and taking part in the sweat lodge or a vision quest. For the Dakota, religion is a matter of participation, not theorizing. It is not a thing written about in books but a thing to be vitally experienced with others in the community.

Since that encounter in the Yankton Dakota community, I've come to notice other religions that do not have creeds (statements of belief) or theologies. Buddhism, at least in most of its varieties, seems to operate that way. If you ask Buddhists for a statement of belief, they will give you the four noble truths, none of which even mentions a divine being. If you press them beyond that, they may give you the same knowing smile that I received from the Dakota chief, indicating that you are asking the wrong question. Taoism is another Asian religion that seems to want to avoid belief articulations, warning that "the tao that can be spoken is not the eternal tao, the tao that can be named is not the eternal name" (Lao Tzu, 1974, ch. 1). Ancient Hellenic religion was rich in story and other artistic expression but did not articulate anything like a system of beliefs. Judaism is also an example of a noncreedal and largely nontheological religion. Like the Dakota community, the focus for Judaism seems to be on being a community of practice: reading the stories, singing the songs, eating the meal, gathering as a community of remembrance. There are many more faith communities for whom belief is not religiously focal. It would make an interesting project to explore them.

B. Even Religions That Seem to Be Belief-Focused May Not Be as Much as They Seem

At the beginning of this chapter, I suggested that we are inclined to think of religion as belief because of our exposure to Christianity as the paradigm that has shaped our thinking. Belief certainly does play a central and important role in Christianity. Most Christian worship services include reciting a creed as part of their process. If you visit a Christian seminary, you are likely to find thousands of books on theology, most of which are attempts to articulate a statement of belief central to the faith.

But belief is not focal for all Christians. If you visit a Quaker meeting and engage the participants in conversation afterward, you are likely to find a deep lack of concern about beliefs. It's not that those in attendance have no beliefs. What you're very likely to find is that they have the widest variety of beliefs imaginable. As one participant said to me, "Here you will find theists and atheists and agnostics, people with fairly traditional Protestant beliefs and people who have blended together Christianity and Buddhism or Shinto or something else. We tolerate a wide variety of belief and non-belief because we don't think it's all that important. What's essential for us is experience and practice."

Kathleen Norris, noted poet and essayist, recounts her coming back to church after many years of absence. The problem with her return to church was that she was sure that belief was necessary. In her book *Amazing Grace*, she writes:

> Other people had it, I did not. And for a long time, even though I was attracted to church, I was convinced that I did not belong there, because my beliefs were not solid, set in stone. When I first stumbled on the Benedictine abbey where I am now an oblate, I was surprised to find the monks so unconcerned with my weighty doubts and intellectual frustration over Christianity. What interested them more was my desire to come to their worship, the liturgy of the hours. (Norris, 1998, 62, 63)

Later in the same book, Norris recounts her own struggles with the creeds she was called on to recite in church. She finally came to realize that the apparent unconcern of the monks for her beliefs and doubts was really bothering her. In some ways, she felt they were not taking her and her struggles seriously. It then occurred to her that this self-focus was the source of her problem and that worship was a way beyond it. She writes: "Praise of God is the entire reason for worship. It is the opposite of self-consciousness" (63).

At the point of her writing, Norris had become an occasional lay preacher in the Presbyterian church. She writes about her current way of regarding the creeds:

> I came to consider that the creeds are a form of speaking in tongues. And in that sense they are a relief from the technological jargon we hear on a daily basis. Now when I am preaching . . . I usually select the Nicene Creed, because then no one can pretend to know exactly what it is they are saying. "God of God, Light of Light, Very God of Very God." It gives me great pleasure to hear a church full of respectable people suddenly start to talk like William Blake. Only the true literalists are left out, refusing to play the game. (206)

In another of her books, *Dakota: A Spiritual Biography,* Norris writes: "We go to church in order to sing, and theology is secondary" (91).

Another author echoes Norris's view. Phillip Clayton, a contemporary theologian, writes:

> Like many other people, I was taught that the only route to being a disciple of Jesus—and indeed, the only route to any serious Christian identity—was *believe, behave, belong.* . . . So we first sit down and try to believe the Christian propositions that people tell us we should believe. . . . Like many others, I have found these marching orders to be the cause of rather continuous guilt. (Clayton, 2009, pp. 39–40)

By contrast, Clayton goes on to say, "A postmodern understanding of religion in general, and of Christian discipleship in particular, reverses the order" (40).

C. Assuming That Faith Is Belief-Focused Narrows Our Vision

The first reason to challenge the assumption that believing is the focal act of religion is that it neglects and excludes many religions and many people within religions. If we begin with the assumption that belief is focal, then we are very likely to exclude a lot of people who, like Norris, lack such beliefs. The exclusion may be enforced by the community, or it may be, as it was in Norris's case, self-enforced.

The second reason to question the assumption that believing is the focal act of faith is closely related to the first. If we assume that belief is focal, we may miss the importance of other activities and practices in the life of faith, such as storytelling, singing, dancing, eating the communal meal, smoking the pipe, and so forth. Kathleen Norris is, once again, an excellent example of this. As long as she saw belief as focal, her doubts kept her from participating in the activities of worship. As she puts it: "Though I was attracted to church, I was convinced that I did not belong there."

My estimate is that nearly all the once-churched people who do not now participate in religious practice do so because they assume, like Norris, that belief is focal and necessary and they cannot participate because they do not have it. If we could get rid of that assumption, people might be open to performing some religious experiments. Try sitting silently with the Quakers for an hour practicing receptiveness. Try (if you dare) participating in a Dakota sweat lodge. Participate in a celebratory meal remembering a story in the Jewish tradition. Read or hear or act out a sacred story, and consider how it might change the way you look at life and the world. Sing in a choir performing one of Bach's oratorio masterpieces. Dance, in your own clumsy way, at a friend's naming ceremony. Stand in a circle, holding hands around the grave side of a dear friend or family member. What you may learn is that the experience is moving and even life changing even though it may never result in any statement of belief.

When I was a grad student at Yale, I talked an atheist friend of mine into attending a Sunday service with me at the Yale chapel. I think the fact that William Sloan Coffin Jr. was the preacher had much to do with my friend's willingness to come. Back in those days, Rev. Coffin was getting a lot of media attention for his protests against the Vietnam War. My friend sat through the whole service, attending to what was said but showing little enthusiasm for it. The service ended with a baptism during which Rev. Coffin picked up the child and held her in his hands high above his head as he walked out into the congregation. He shouted out, "Please welcome Cynthia Marie, child of God, into the family." My friend sprang to his feet, leading what turned out to be a standing ovation. Afterward, he said, "That was beautiful—thanks for inviting me along. But I still can't believe all that stuff."

Assuming faith is belief focused can also limit the range of a person's reactions to stories he or she encounters. In 2006, when Dan Brown's novel *The Da Vinci Code* was released, I got calls from three different journalists. Basically, the phone exchanges went like this:

J: Have you read *The Da Vinci Code*?
T: Yes, I have.
J: What did you think of it?
T: I thought it was an interesting mystery, a well-crafted story that held my interest all the way through.
J: Yes, but what did you think of the claims that were made about Jesus and Mary Magdalene and the Catholic Church?
T: It didn't, to my knowledge, make any claims about any of those things. It is a work of fiction.
J: In other words, you didn't believe what Brown said?
T: Look, Brown is a novelist; there's no reason to suppose that *he* believed the things stated in the novel. Why should I, or anyone else, regard these as claims to be believed or disbelieved if the author doesn't even regard them that way? It's a story. It should be read as a story and enjoyed as a story.
J: So, do you want to go on record as agreeing with Brown or disagreeing with him?
T: I want to go on record as refusing to answer your question because it is so stupid. A good journalist shouldn't . . .
J: Click!

Why were so many people upset and even made irate by Brown's novel? My guess is it has something to do with a widespread tendency in our culture to suppose that believing and disbelieving are the only alternatives when one encounters topics even vaguely related to religious matters.

I used to have an elderly landlady who wrote letters of advice to the characters in her favorite soap operas—for example, "Can't you see that he's not the right man for you? You should marry Tony, not that creep Edward." and "You'll never be happy with her. She's not faithful to you; she's just out to get your money. Can't you see that?" These were not fan letters to the actors; they were letters *to the characters*. For whatever reason, she did not seem capable of distinguishing between fiction and actuality. At the time, I thought this was a harmless characteristic of a peculiar old lady. I now think it may be much more widespread, a confusion that is fairly common in our culture.

D. Believing Is Not an Intentional Activity

We often enjoin and encourage people to take their religion seriously. Godparents in many Christian communities promise to encourage and enable the faith development of the children they sponsor. We promise to bring them to church, to encourage their reading of Scripture and their participation in the sacraments, and so forth. All of these things we can enjoin and encourage the young person to do. What we cannot sensibly do is enjoin them to believe. Believing is not something that can be done intentionally and deliberately. I can't say, "Tomorrow I will change my beliefs. From then on I will believe in the meaninglessness of life and the universe." I either believe that or I do not. I can't say, "Beginning tomorrow, I will believe that Zeus made my daughter pregnant." No matter how many rewards or threats someone presents me with, I just can't believe that.

Lewis Carroll, in his masterpiece "Alice through the Looking Glass," presents us with the following bit of sublime nonsense:

> "Let's consider your age to begin with—[the Queen said] how old are you?"
>
> "I'm seven and a half, exactly [said Alice]."
>
> "You needn't say 'exactly,' the Queen remarked, "I can believe it without that. Now I'll give you something to believe. I'm just one hundred and one, five months and a day."
>
> "I can't believe *that*," said Alice.
>
> "Can't you?" the Queen said in a pitying tone. "Try again: draw a long breath, and shut your eyes."
>
> Alice laughed, "There's no use trying," she said: "one can't believe impossible things."
>
> "I daresay you haven't had much practice," said the Queen. "When I was your age, I always did it for half an hour a day. Why, sometimes I'd believe as many as six impossible things before breakfast."

One can't believe something by deciding to do it. One can't believe by trying hard to do it, not even after taking a long breath and closing one's eyes. Martin Luther, in his Small Catechism, states, "I cannot by my own power or strength believe in Jesus Christ nor come to him. But the Holy Spirit has called me through the gospel, enlightened me with his gifts." Beliefs, like doubts, are not really something we choose. We "find ourselves" believing or doubting in spite of our wishes and intentions. It might be appropriate to talk about "falling into belief" or "falling into doubt" as we do about "falling in love." We don't really have much choice in the matter. Since belief is not chosen, one cannot really be blamed for the beliefs or doubts one has. One may be blamed for believing on bad or insufficient reasons. But if someone I know finds something unbelievable, there is no point in my saying, "But you ought to believe it." I may, however, give a person reasons to believe something. It is the force of reasons (or the lack thereof) that moves us to belief or doubt. So, we find ourselves saying, "I used to believe X but then I discovered Y. I now find X no longer believable. I may wish to believe something but find it impossible to do so." Religious practice, on the other hand, is intentional. I can promise to read a sacred text and then do it. I can promise to partake in a religious ritual and then do so. But I can't promise to believe something. Either something is believable to me or it isn't. The supporting reasons make something believable, not my act of will.

So, propositional believing is neither an intentional nor a willed act. Yet faith, at least to some degree, seems to be such. May we conclude then that faith is more a mode of participation, association, and practice than it is a mode of belief?

E. Believing is Too Cognitive and Too Logo-Centric to Be the Focal Act of Faith

I often ask my students how many believe that zagruks scapulate glaucously. None raises a hand. So I teasingly conclude, "So, you all *doubt* that zagruks scapulate glaucously?" Usually, some student will point out the stupidity of my assertion by saying, "We can't either believe or doubt a proposition we don't understand." She will, of course, be right. What this implies is that if belief is religiously focal, so is understanding. If I lack understanding, I can't have faith. Understanding is, at least, a necessary condition for propositional belief.

If I claim to believe in the communion of saints, I need to be able to explain to someone what this means. If I claim to believe that God the father, Jesus, and the Holy Spirit are all one being in three persons, I need to be able to explain what, exactly, it is I am believing. In other words, explicit theology is a prerequisite of propositional belief. If belief is, in turn, the focal act of faith, then a level of theological education is a prerequisite of faith. If belief is the focal act of faith, then systematic theologians are the paradigm case of the faithful. But most people, many theologians among them, think that's ridiculous. Can't simple and uneducated people and children be exemplars of the faith? I would certainly say so. If we think of the inspiring exemplars of the faith, who are they? Theologians? Doctrinal historians? Not likely. Beliefs are too propositional, too logo-centric, and too cognitive to be the focal act of faith.

The problem with being belief focused is that we are likely to regard every statement as something we either believe or doubt, that is, as either credible or incredible. The other possibility is that the statement is noncredible, that is, that some other response than belief or doubt is called for. I may be inspired by a poem from Mary Oliver. I may be provoked to deep questioning by a short story from John Updike. I may have my life transformed by a novel from Dostoevsky. And all of these things may happen without raising the question of whether to believe or to not believe what I am reading or hearing.

F. Many Serious Thinkers Have Suggested Other Things as Being Religiously Focal

Many different thinkers could be provided to illustrate this point, but it should suffice to give a few brief examples.

First, Søren Kierkegaard, a nineteenth-century Danish Christian thinker, argued that faith is not the opposite of doubt but something that actually requires doubt. Doubt, as well as cognitive confusion, actually lights and feeds the existential passion of faith, which Kierkegaard understood as a kind of ultimate life commitment. For Kierkegaard, belief is neither focal nor required for faith but, in a sense, stands in the way of it. What is required on the part of the Christian writer, Kierkegaard maintains, is not to make Christianity more believable but to focus and inflame the passion of faith.

Second, Paul Tillich, a twentieth-century German American theologian, defined faith as ultimate concern. Many people who have ultimate concerns (justice, equality, truth, authenticity) do not consider themselves religious. Tillich, however, is willing to take them, rather than many "religious" persons, as the paradigm of faith.

Third, Frederick Ferré, a twentieth-century American philosopher, argued that the defining genus of religion is valuing. Religion is intensive valuing of comprehensive values. "Intensive" describes the subjective side of faith, that is, how we value something religiously. "Comprehensive" describes the objective side of faith, that is, what it is that is valued. If we lack the first, our valuing is indifferent and apathetic. If we lack the second, our valuing may be intense but trivial, like a hobby or an obsession.

Finally, Louis Pojman, the twentieth-century American philosopher cited in the preface, suggests that hope, rather than belief, may be the religiously focal activity. While hope requires a belief in the possibility that something can be true, it does not imply a belief that it will be true; in fact, hope requires a high degree of uncertainty. Moreover, hoping requires the making of a commitment, it is motivational, and it requires the willingness to run some risk. Pojman thinks these features of hope resemble much more what we admire in the religious person than believing does.

The fact that some noted thinkers do not make the assumption that belief is religiously focal does not prove that the assumption is wrong. But it does provide us with a reason to question it. Very often, we make assumptions because we can't think of any other way things might be. This section bears testimony to the fact that there are other ways, some of them quite interesting.

A Thought Experiment

When I was at Oxford University in the 1970s and 1980s, there were a number of odd organizations. One I remember in particular was the Society for the Pursuit of Lost Causes. They met every fortnight planning strategies for the recovery of Britain's lost American colonies. Another I encountered was a small group of persons who had in common that they shared a particular belief—that humans came to this planet from another place in outer space.

All members of the latter group shared that belief, though they disagreed somewhat about the details. Most members believed that this human earth colony was one among several experiments sent out to habitable planets and that those who sent (or brought) us here at least periodically observe us. There was a good deal of disagreement over whether these beings constantly observe us, like psychology students observing rats in a lab, or only occasionally observe how we're doing—for example, once every century or so. There was also some disagreement about whether those who sent us here are themselves human or some kind of super race. A couple members related to me that they believed that our cosmic observers place bets on our survival and development. On the great stats board in the cosmic equivalent of Las Vegas are some interesting questions: "How long until the human race annihilates itself?" "How long until they use up all the earth's nonrenewable resources?" "Will they learn to live peacefully with one another or is war part of the permanent human condition?" "How long until they discover that we're observing them and begin to communicate with us?" Bets are placed daily, and the odds change correspondingly.

The Oxford group was somewhat diverse. Most of the members were male academics ranging in age from twenty-five to eighty years old, though there was also a smaller group of women (mostly in their forties and fifties) and quite a few "townies," including the deputy chief constable of the city of Oxford. Two of the members were from Africa, and two were from India. The group met monthly to debate and discuss and then retire to a local pub for a pint of beer. On the few occasions when I attended, vigorous debate addressed what the group should be named. All seemed to agree that the previous name, the Colonists, was no longer appropriate.

The question I would like you to consider is this: is there any reason to think that this group is a religion? It is certainly a group focused by a common belief, and the belief has something to do with the human genesis, the human story, extraterrestrial beings, and our relation to an otherworldly reality. Why would we doubt that it is a religion? What is missing from it that, if present, would incline us to call it a religion? I'd like to call attention to the absence of four things.

First, there is no sense of the sacred. There is no sacred place, no sacred object, no sacred times, no holy days, no pilgrimages, no focus for worship or contemplation. There is no symbol or sacred text either. Some suggested that the ancestors, or "the initiating generation," is, in some sense, worshipped, but I don't think that's so. Most of the members simply regard them as a group that brought us here as an experiment. These "founders" are not assumed to be beneficent or praiseworthy, just curious enough to run an experiment, and we are it, or at least part of it.

Second, the focal story this group tells does not seem to have any transformative power. It is not a paradigm for understanding the world or life. It is not expected that people hearing this story will live transformed lives.

Also, there is no ritual. There are no hymns, no celebrations, no holidays. The only thing performed regularly is the reading of the minutes of the last gathering, which consist almost entirely of the topics that were discussed and which pub all retired to at the end. The drinking of the pint may be as much ritual as this group can manage.

Finally, there is no ethic. The story does not inspire a particular pattern of responsibility or behavior (except drinking beer) or a particular appreciation for the earth or for other humans either. There is nothing the members are obliged to do or obliged to avoid doing. The only requirement is believing that the human race came to this planet from another place and that there are humans (or humanoids) elsewhere in the cosmos observing us.

If any of these four conditions were present, there would be some reason to think that a religion was being practiced. If all of them were present, there would be, I think, sufficient reason to draw such a conclusion.

What is the point of this reflection? It is to demonstrate that a set of beliefs—even a set of beliefs about our beginnings, our cosmic situation, our future, and even an otherworldly reality related to us—is not sufficient to make something a religion. Something moves toward being a religion when the set of beliefs or the informing story starts to shape our understanding of ourselves, the world, and others. A belief or story becomes religious when it informs a way of seeing that informs a way of living. A religious story is not just a believed story; it is a life-informing story.

James Carse on the Religious Case against Belief

James Carse, in his 2008 book *The Religious Case against Belief*, wants to distinguish clearly between the human interest in religion and the human inclination toward systems of belief. He characterizes religion as a *communitas*, a culture, as opposed to a *civitas*, a political system, structure, or institution. He says that *communitas* is characterized by the fact that it endures for centuries, sometimes even for millennia, and that it seems to tolerate and endure many particular social and historical manifestations.

Religions, he argues, are to be distinguished from belief systems in several respects. First, belief systems always spring up as opposed to some other belief system. If the opposing system dies out, so does most of the eros of the belief system. Religions do not arise in this way, nor are they dependent on others to which they are opposed. Carse writes: "[Beliefs] are essentially dyadic. Every offered belief has its distinctly objectionable opposite. . . . For

30 | Questioning Assumptions

that reason, questions, even when genuinely asked, seem to be little more than triggers for answers already prepared" (2008, 186).

Second, religions embody the perennial posing of the deepest questions. They are what Carse calls "a conjunction of questions" (191). Belief systems are attempts to answer these questions. Third, belief systems end a conversation. Religions are a conversation. Fourth, belief systems are explicit verbalizations. Religions continually point to what lies behind language. Fifth, belief systems are formulated. Religions are sung, danced, and expressed architecturally and artistically. Just like a great poem often moves us to write a poem in response, so religions call forth and enlarge our creative capacities, to perform an act of interpretive resonance with the tradition. Beliefs call forth repetition, not creative interpretation. Interpretation, or "revisionism," is anathema to the true believer.

Sixth, for religions, the fundamental texts are deep and open. For belief, texts are narrow and limited in meaning. Using Islam as an example, Carse writes: "Suppose, however, that Muslims come to a broad consensus on how the Qur'an is to be interpreted; were they to do so, they would have substituted the consensus for the text itself. The Qur'an would then have become dispensable. At best it would serve as a proof text for one or another of their beliefs" (203).

Finally, the ideal case of a belief system is the achievement of orthodoxy. The ideal religion, on the other hand, is the one that nourishes the richest range of disagreement within itself. "Believers," Carse states, "are terrified by genuine expressions of religion" (206). Carse congratulates both Judaism and Christianity for the ways they have made that possible and, of course, also condemns them for those times in their history when heterodoxy has not been allowed. He fears that Christianity is now entering such a time. He states: "It is less a religion than a belief system. Where are its poets?" (207). About Buddhism, Carse writes:

> When the dying Buddha assured his grieving friends that his body would decay . . . he was asked whether he would live on after death. He answered in effect: we cannot say the Buddha lives on; we cannot say he does not; we cannot say he both lives on and does not. On the one hand he emphasizes the reality of his death, on the other the utter impossibility of understanding it. This open-ended, or what I have called horizontal, way of thinking then penetrates every aspect of Buddhism (p. 209).

Carse notes that almost all contemporary authors who attack religion attack it as if it were a belief system. They alone cannot be faulted, however, because many of the defenders who argue back make the same assumption, as does the general culture. As Carse admits: "The world is far more attracted to belief systems than to religion as I have described it" (209). Yet he is borne up by the hope that there will always be poets and that they cannot help but sing.

G. The Term *Believe* Is Not Univocal

You may have heard the story about two Harvard philosophers, Josiah Royce and William James, walking along a country road having an argument. As will happen with philosophers, one topic led to another until finally they were talking about matters theological and what the common man believed about such matters. At that moment, just such a man, a Yankee local, came over the hill walking toward them. The philosophers said to him, "Please, sir, if you would answer a question for us you could help us settle an argument." The man stopped and nodded assent. "Tell us, do you believe in infant baptism?" The man looked them over with a puzzled eye and replied, "Believe in it? Shucks, I've even seen it happen."

One can imagine other humorous miscommunications based on the confusion of senses of the word *believe:*

"Do you believe in premarital sex?"
"Yes, in fact I think it's quite common."

"Do you believe in horoscopes?"
"Sure, there's one in today's paper."

Sometimes one may hear a question about belief and not know which sense is being asked about:

"Do you believe in acupuncture?"

"Do you believe in romantic love?"

"Do you believe in universal health care?"

Clearly, there are different senses to the word *believe* and different ways in which someone may believe something. The philosopher story would provide us no entertainment if that were not so. But even though sophisticated people realize this, they still frequently confuse themselves and others by not clearly distinguishing among <u>different senses of the word *believe*</u> and the differing acts we call believing.

The assumption that believing is religiously focal often overlooks the fact that *belief* and *believe* are not univocal. In fact, a wide range of actions falls under forms of the word. Let us consider a few different uses and meanings the term has in order to show what confusion can occur if these meanings are not distinguished.

Belief-That and Belief-In

<u>The most common differentiation is between "belief that" and "belief in."</u> In the 2008 Democratic presidential primaries, I had several acquaintances who were supporting the candidacy of Ohio congressman Dennis Kucinic. They liked his values, they trusted him, and they were willing to commit their money and efforts to his campaign, yet not one of them *believed that* he was going to win. *Belief in* seems to have a variety of species, trusting, valuing, and hoping among them. Of course, Kucinic's supporters also had *beliefs that*: they believed that they knew what he stood for, they believed that he wouldn't suddenly change his fundamental values, and so forth. Usually, we distinguish between these two kinds of believing without confusion. But sometimes *beliefs in* get expressed as *beliefs that*. At a political convention, a person may be nominated for office. The person making the nomination may say, "I am proud to place in nomination the next governor of the glorious state of Ohio, Squeaky Clean." The person may nominate Ms. Clean without actually believing that she will become the next governor. Introducing her in that way is meant to help convince the audience to get on the bandwagon for her. The nomination, which I take as an articulation of a *belief in* this candidate, is expressed as though it is a *belief that* she will win.

The fight song of my college alma mater has a line that goes "Maroon and gold, our colors, [will] see victory today." My guess is that many thousands of supporters have sung that song over the years without actually believing that their school would win. We *hope* that we will win, we *believe in* the school, showing support for it in a variety of ways, but that doesn't imply that we *believe that* it will defeat every opponent it encounters.

I believe in my doctor. I trust him to take care of me. That does not imply that I believe he will always cure my ills or that he will never make a mistake.

My belief in him is a belief in his values and that my welfare is among those things he cares about.

The Declaration of Independence contains the following lines:

> We hold these truths to be self-evident, that all men are created equal, that they are endowed by their Creator with certain unalienable rights, that among these are life, liberty and the pursuit of happiness. That to secure these rights, governments are instituted among men, deriving their just powers from the consent of the governed.

Here we get the clearly stated belief that all men are created equal. What sort of thing were the founders doing when they claimed to believe this? They make it perfectly clear that there is no doubt about this. The proposition is so clearly true as to be "self-evident." It is also so firmly believed that they are willing to put their "lives, fortunes, and sacred honor" at risk by signing on to this document. Yet, I am quite sure that if you asked any of the men signing this document whether they thought that all men were equal in any measurable way they would have admitted that we are not. We are unequal in size, unequal in wealth, unequal in intelligence, unequal in talents and gifts, unequal in strength and health. Since they all certainly knew this, what were they affirming by making the "self-evident" claim that all men are created equal? Are they claiming that this should be true, even if it is not? I doubt it. The presence of many inequalities make our society richer, stronger, and more flexible. A society of clones was not the founders' goal. What then did they mean?

Some people would say that although the statement sounds as if it is affirming an empirical claim—that all men are, in fact, created equal—it is not. To regard it in such a way is to misunderstand it. Instead, the statement is making a religious or metaphysical claim: that all men are equal in the eyes of God or in the eyes of the law or in the domain of human rights, and so forth. They are claiming the self-evident truth of this statement in some domain that is not empirically verifiable, a domain that serves as a foundation for ethics and politics. From this truth, many things will follow, including an argument for representative democracy, a bill of rights, the eventual end to slavery, the eventual enfranchisement of women, and so forth. So the domain that is being talked about is not an unimportant one, but neither is it an empirical one.

Are religious statements of belief like this? There is some reason to think so. Very often, religious beliefs are unshakably held in spite of what seems to be much contrary evidence. Socrates affirms: "No harm can come to a good man either in this life or the next." Yet, he is on the verge of being imprisoned and put to death. Does he mean that no harm can be done to the *soul* of a good man? Where is this carried out if not either "in this life or the next?" In what world, in other words, is this statement true? St. Paul states: "We know that in everything God works for good with those who love him, who are called according to his purpose" (Rom. 8:25). Does the suffering and death of the Christian martyrs not count against this? In what world is St. Paul's claim true? About what domain is the Christian speaking when he affirms this? What exactly does believing this amount to?

Beliefs—Epistemic and Pragmatic

One possible response to these paradoxes is to point again to the different meanings of the word *belief* and the different senses in which something may be believed. It should at least be clear that some confusion exists about this and that care must be taken in using this term. Besides the distinction between "belief in" and "belief that," there is another distinction that is no less important—the distinction between epistemic and pragmatic beliefs. *Epistemic beliefs* are beliefs in the truth of a claim or proposition. *Pragmatic beliefs* are beliefs we act on. We can tell a person's epistemic beliefs by hearing what she says; we see a person's pragmatic beliefs by seeing what she does.

Martin Luther comments in one section of his "Table Talk" that if he were to find out that the world would end tomorrow, he would in spite of that go out today and plant a tree. This action would be unremarkable if he did not believe (epistemically) that the world would end. If, on the other hand, he believes what he is told, then his action is a testimony to a radical hope that he expresses by the way he lives.

A few weeks ago, I was interviewed by a visitor to our campus. She asked me why I felt a calling to be a teacher. Among my comments was that I teach in order to help my students become more critical thinkers, and I do that because I think the world desperately needs more critical thinkers. If one looks at the behavior of humans in the last century, one sees a horrible series of wars, fueled by nationalistic, ethnic, class, and religious chauvinism, plus environmental destructiveness and waste on a global scale. We desperately need to question the assumptions by which we've been living and acting. The interviewer asked, "So you believe that the human species is capable of the change necessary in time to avert global destruction?" I answered, "No, I'm not at all optimistic. Ever so many evidences point toward our not learning how to live sustainably and peaceably. Greed, chauvinism and war seem to be hardwired into our nature." She responded, "But then why do you continue to make the effort?" I quoted Luther's comment and stated, "Even if I believed that the human race was doomed to destroy both itself and the planet, I would still continue to teach critical thinking."

William James, in his famous essay "The Will to Believe," uses the example of a man caught on a mountainside in a blinding snowstorm. The man doesn't know the way down the mountain and can't see more than two steps in front of him. He has no grounds for belief. He does not know the way, and he doesn't know if he will survive. Yet, he knows that if he does nothing and stays where he is he will freeze to death. Epistemically he is filled with doubt, yet pragmatically he courageously walks on.

College friends of mine who worked as ambulance drivers and medics told many stories about picking up auto accident or shooting victims. They treated and transported them without much hope that the victims would survive the trip to the emergency room. They said, "But we always act on the assumption that we'll get them there in time to be treated and saved. What we believe [epistemically] is irrelevant."

In our courts of law, we make the presumption of innocence—that is, we presume that an accused person is innocent until he or she can be proven beyond reasonable doubt to be guilty. Many times, we do that in spite of the fact that we may believe the accused to be guilty. The police may believe it, the prosecuting attorney may believe it, even the judge and the defense attorney may believe it, but all of them must act on the presumption of innocence. It is not a requirement in any case that the defense attorney believe (epistemically) the accused. But it is a requirement that he or she acts (pragmatically) on such a presumption.

Epistemic beliefs are defended by giving reasons to think the belief is true. Pragmatic beliefs are defended by talking not about evidences or probabilities but about actions and ways of living. Epistemic beliefs are about what we think is true in the world. Pragmatic beliefs are expressions of our deepest values, hopes, and concerns as well as our personal identities.

I recently received as a gift a book titled *This I Believe (2004)*. It is a collection of short essays, some of which were originally radio broadcasts back in the 1950s. The series was revived by National Public Radio just a few years ago. The book contains statements by Albert Einstein, Martha Graham,

Leonard Bernstein, and Eleanor Roosevelt as well as by such significant contemporaries as Bill Gates, Oprah Winfrey, and recent presidents. As one reads through these two- to three-page pieces, it becomes obvious that almost no one is writing about epistemic beliefs, that is, about some proposition they believe to be true. Everyone writes about what motivates and orients their lives, that is, their pragmatic beliefs:

"I believe in people and the good people can do."

"I believe you are what you give. It's by spending yourself in love that you become someone."

"I believe that with gifts and good fortune comes a responsibility to give back to the world."

"I don't believe in boredom. The world is infinitely rich. The person who doesn't know that is the one who lives in poverty no matter how much he/she possesses."

"I don't believe in going half way. If something's worth doing it's worth my full effort."

Are religious beliefs like this? Are they more like pragmatic beliefs than like epistemic beliefs? If so, why do we continue to challenge and defend them as if they were epistemic beliefs? Why operate on such an assumption? Do we suppose that pragmatic beliefs are worth very little and that only epistemic beliefs are important and worthy? Where would we have gotten such a prejudice?

"Believe" Has Not Always Meant What It Most Commonly Means Now

Wilfred Cantwell Smith, in his book *Faith and Belief* (1979), tells us: "Literally and originally, 'to believe' meant 'to hold dear': virtually to love. . . . This is what its German equivalent *belieben* still means today. . . . *Belieben*, then, means to treat as *lieb*, to consider lovely, to like, to wish for, to choose" (104).

Belief has come over the years to mean something more like "to consider or judge to be true." Now we can easily imagine the confusion that can occur—even for one who, like Kathleen Norris, attempts to be a believer—for someone who supposes that belief can be understood only in the "to think true" sense when originally it may have meant something more like "to hold dear," or "to commit one's life to."

There are many things that I hold dear and that have shaped my life that I do not consider to be true. There are works of fiction or characters in fiction that have shaped and changed my life. This has occurred in spite of the fact that I have all along known them to be works of fiction. I needn't consider a story to be factual or a character to be historical for that to occur. Gulley Jimson has, and continues, to influence my life, yet I have known from the beginning that he was a creation of the imagination of the author Joyce Cary and later of the actor Alec Guinness. If some historian were to provide incontrovertible proof that the Socrates of Plato's dialogues was nothing like the historical Socrates, that he was a creation of Plato's imagination, it wouldn't bother me. It is not the historical Socrates I believe in, but the one Plato so vividly presents us. So obviously, to say that I am a believer in Socrates is not to say that I believe the dialogues to be historically accurate. For the kind of belief I have, that is beside the point. I can imagine someone saying something similar about Gautama Siddhartha or Jesus or the prophet Amos, for example.

Many Christians are very concerned to say that they believe their religious statements in a literal, factual, and empirical sense. To say that this sense may not be focal and that it is unnecessary is to ask them to give up what seems to them the very essence of belief. For many, the only sense of *believe* that's worth talking about is the literal "believe that" sense, and the only kinds of things worth believing are things that are true in the empirical, factual sense. Although I know that this occurs and perhaps is even very common, I just do not understand it. It isn't so much that I doubt it as that I just don't find it very interesting. I am much more interested in the religious beliefs that guide and shape a person's life than I am in what scientific or historical or otherwise factual proposition they judge to be true.

How Should We Handle This Problem?

Earlier in the writing process, I had considered titling this section "Is Believing What Believers Really Do?" I liked the way it focused the issue, but I decided it might occasion more confusion than necessary. How do we handle the confusions about belief and its role that we have uncovered here?

We could go a couple of different directions. We could stop talking about belief when we mean to talk about faith. We could stop assuming that faith equals belief and stop asserting that belief is the basic and focal act of faith. Or we could distinguish between different senses of *belief* whenever we use the term and make it perfectly clear which of several senses we intend to use. Do we mean "belief that" or "belief in"? Do we mean belief in the epistemic sense or belief in the pragmatic sense? Or do we intend to use *belief* in some other sense altogether?

Whichever of these paths we take, I think there are certain guidelines anyone doing philosophy of religion should follow:

- We should stop making the assumption that belief is the focal or crucial act of faith. If we wish to contend that belief is or ought to be focal, we need to realize that an explanation needs to be given and an argument needs to be made. We can't any longer just presume that belief is the focal act of faith.
- We should be aware that faith may not be exactly the same in different religious traditions and that in some of them belief plays hardly any role at all.
- We should be aware that the word *belief* had and still has a variety of uses and meanings and that it is very easy to use it in one sense while assuming one is using it in another.
- We should be open to the possibility that something other than belief in the epistemic sense is and ought to be the focal act of faith. Believing may not be the best description for what believers do.

FROM THE CLASSROOM: STUDENT QUESTIONS & RESPONSES

Q: I have trouble even imagining what faith without belief would look like. I would say that belief is at the very foundation of faith, and I think many people would agree.

R: I'm sure you're right about what many people would say. We have been brought up to think this way influenced in large part by the dominance of Christianity in our culture. But reflect for a moment about what believing is. Isn't it, for a Christian, some combination of thinking about Jesus, having a vivid image of him in one's mind, recalling the things that he did, reflecting on the things that he taught, perhaps reciting prayers, psalms, passages from Scripture, and parts of the liturgy? These are the things that we do when we talk about believing. But of course they are not believing in the narrow sense of the word. They are, however, most certainly an important part of the life of faith. Although it sounds kind of stupid to say it, I think there's some reason to doubt whether believing is what believers actually do.

Q: What are we supposed to do with the doubts that we have? Silence them? Stifle them? Deny them? Try very hard to refute them? Those are the answers my pastors and teachers at church have urged on me. But I have found they don't really work. What are you saying—that doubts are OK?

R: I would say that asking hard questions is part of the life of faith. Faith is not inimical to critical thinking, openness, imagination, and doubt. All of these can occasion tremendous personal growth, and that is part of the life of faith. Any faith that makes us become smaller, narrower, more two-dimensional persons should be suspect. Faith is not pretending that we have no doubts.

Once having admitted our own doubts, then maybe we can go on to see that belief is not the main part of faith, particularly if it's a belief that has to be, in a sense, forced on a person. I hope you'll come to see that in the process of reading this text.

Q: Is it really true that we cannot believe a statement that we don't understand? In many of the science classes I've taken, I have been told things by textbooks and teachers that I didn't completely understand, yet I believed them because they were being taught me in the science class.

R: Fascinating comment! It points to an interesting muddle in our language. If someone asked me whether I believe in Boyle's law, I might just answer that I do even though I cannot remember precisely what Boyle's law is. I may remember only that it had something to do with the pressure of gases. Under those circumstances, I think it's a mistake to say that I *believe* Boyle's law. What I probably should say is that I have confidence in my teacher or in the science education I received. I may also have confidence that *if* I understood Boyle's law, I would believe it. That may be what's going on in a religious context as well. I may say, "I believe in the communion of saints," and really mean by that, "If I understood the statement, I think I would believe it."

Q: Why do you refuse to believe that virgin births and coming back from the dead really happen?

R: Thanks for asking this question because I hope it will be an occasion to clear up a confusion that many readers may have at this point. First of all, I don't recall ever claiming that such things never happen. We live in a world where a lot of really weird things happen. So, you are making a large assumption in your question. But, more important, the fact that really weird things can happen is not the focal part of religious faith. The question is, do such occurrences have a religious significance? I can believe that a twelve-year-old girl who has never had sex suddenly finds herself pregnant. In fact, I know of a case like that. But I don't see this as necessarily a miracle or as the heart of a life-orienting story. I just see it as a really unusual event. The mistake is to assume that this is what religious people believe, namely, that really unusual events occurred. Faith begins, it seems to me, in our seeing the will and love of God manifest in an event, whether that event is something usual or something unusual. When I see the world shaped by such a revelation, then something religious has occurred.

Resurrection becomes a focal part of faith, not for someone who believes that weird events occur but for someone who, like St. Paul, saw in Jesus dying and rising the theme and pattern for his own daily dying and rising. Paul's faith changes the way he sees his own life. For him, resurrection is not only a past event but also one that occurs in the present and future tenses. A mere belief that Jesus survived his crucifixion does not do that.

Q: When I have told my friends about your argument, many respond that belief is absolutely essential to faith and is the largest part of it. Are they just wrong? Don't they themselves know whether belief is what they do? You mention posing the question "Is believing what believers really do?" That sounds like a really dumb question, and it sounds like the answer is obvious, in fact true by definition. So how could anybody be so bold as to suggest otherwise?

R: I have to admit that it appears to be an outrageous idea. But, having admitted that it sounds very weird, I still think it's not at all obvious that "believing" in the propositional, epistemic sense is at the heart of faith. All I ask is that people stop and question this very common and widespread assumption.

But your question raises a deeper issue: do we always have a clear idea about what we ourselves are doing? Let me suggest an analogy. If you ask someone to explain how to balance on a slow-moving bicycle, you will get a lot of very bad answers. People will say things like "You switch your weight from side to side and maintain balance," or "You balance by moving your shoulders up and down," or "You balance by swinging your butt from side to side." None of these are the true description of what these people really do. People can balance the bike in practice, but they can't accurately describe what they are doing when they do it.

A friend of mine worked for a trumpet company in Chicago. Her job was to record what the craftspeople did in the complex process of making a horn—bending tubing, spinning a bell, building the valves, brazing the joints. She found that, although these people were excellent and experienced craftsmen, they couldn't tell her very accurately what they did. They knew how to do it but had never bothered to examine closely exactly what they were doing or how they did it. They had a kind of embodied know-how, but they had a hard time translating it into a coherent account.

Something similar happens in the life of faith. If you ask people what they are doing, the majority will say "believing." But what does this really amount to? My thesis is that there is a better answer, one that is both more helpful and more accurate.

QUESTIONS FOR CRITICAL REFLECTION

1. This section mentions that the assumption of most classes in philosophy of religion (and by most members of our culture) is that belief is the essential part of faith. Why do so many people believe that if there are considerable reasons for thinking otherwise? Why is that assumption so common?

2. Phillip Clayton remarks that making belief primary simply results in making a lot of people feel guilty about not believing. Does that square with your experience? Does "reversing the order" of believing, behaving, and belonging help to solve this problem?

3. Do you know of any religions other than those cited in this chapter that do not seem to be belief focused? Even if most of the religions of the

world were belief focused to the degree that Christianity is, would that settle the issue? Can you speculate about why Christianity is so belief focused? Why does it, of all religions, have a number of creeds, definitions of what beliefs are heretical, volumes of theology, and so forth?

4. What was your reaction to Norris's "crisis of belief"? Do you think she was right initially in supposing that if she didn't believe all the right stuff then she had no business in church? Were the Benedictine monks right in urging her not to worry about it?

5. Can we believe the Nicene Creed without understanding it? Are we being intellectually dishonest if we speak it as if we understood and believed it when we do not? Would we be better off just remaining silent when the creed is spoken?

6. Do you agree that there are lots of people who have left church or other places of worship because they have found they no longer believed its creeds? Should they, like Norris, give it another try? Would it make a difference if, like Wilfred Cantwell Smith in this chapter, we came to think of belief as "holding dear"?

7. Can small children or people of diminished intellectual capacity be among the religiously faithful? Is the paradigm case of faith the highly educated theologian?

8. Why does Carse think that belief is religiously inappropriate and that a religious case needs to be made *against* belief? How does he understand the term *belief*? What does he think is at the heart of being religious if not belief?

9. What conclusion follows from the discovery that the term *believe* is used in so many different ways? Is that a good thing or a failure of language?

10. Is not knowing exactly what one believes a failure or a virtue? Should each of us annually try to write out a credo for ourselves so that we can clearly answer the question "What do you believe?" Or is it okay to leave such things vague and ambiguous?

2. Questioning Assumptions about God's Existence

Assumption 2. The Basic Religious Question Is about the Existence of God

Theistic arguments are framed as arguments about the existence of something—namely, God. The key philosophical question is assumed to be whether the belief that God exists is a rational belief. Philosophers and other thinkers over the ages have presented arguments that agree and disagree. The larger part of the literature in the philosophy of religion consists of such arguments. But are there reasons to question this assumption? I believe there are several.

A. God Is Not a Thing That May or May Not Exist

Imagine two philosophy students deeply embroiled in an argument about the existence of space. One says, "Space is not anything. It is simply the nothing between things that exist. Something can't be nothing and still exist." "The other says, "But that's ridiculous. I traveled three miles to get here this morning. Tomorrow I'll travel thirty miles to go see my girlfriend. Minneapolis is just over a thousand miles away. All of these measurements are measurements of space, so of course space exists." What both are failing to consider is whether "exists" is the proper thing to say about space.

Space is certainly a considerable reality. But is it *a thing that exists*? In some ways, space is such a fundamental reality that we understand the word "*exists*" in terms of it. To exist means *to be* over time in some space. Space and time are dimensions of existence, but it's misleading to say they are things that do (or do not) exist. The debate the philosophy students are pursuing is interminable because it is mis-framed. Rather than asking, "Does space exist?" or "Does time exist?" it would be much more profitable to ask "How are the reality of time and space manifest?" Then we could talk about clocks, calendars, meters and miles, light-years, aging, cosmic expansion, acceleration, speed limits, music, dance, and so forth.

Theistic arguments assume that "Does God exist?" is the right question. But I doubt very much that it is. God is not some thing or class of things, like unicorns or men from Mars, that we can assert or doubt the existence of. God is much too fundamental a reality for that. The creator certainly cannot be a thing in the creation; the ultimate source cannot be an item in the inventory.

Like space and time, it's more appropriate to think of God as a measure of existence rather than a thing that may or may not exist. It seems to me that the theistic arguments (pro and con) have made a category mistake. The parade is not a unit in the parade, the frame is not a thing in the picture, the university is not a building or a department, and the map is not a location on the map.

Returning to the analogy with space and time, we might redirect our inquiry as follows: "How is the reality of God manifest?" How might we answer? As ultimate value, or as Aristotle put it, as the final *telos* (or end) of all action? As the ultimate standard? As ultimate call, challenge, meaning, questioner? As transformer, redeemer, empowerer? As superlative truth, beauty, goodness, justice, wisdom? As what A. N. Whitehead meant when he talked about the poet of the universe?

A critical reader may object: "But don't all of these descriptions of the manifestation of the reality of God presuppose the existence of God?" My response would be to say, "Be careful what you are doing and assuming here—for example, that something cannot possibly have reality that does not exist, and that only existing things can have the power to focus and transform lives." Neither of these assumptions is true. Space and time (among other things) are exceptions to the first assumption. A discussion of the second assumption follows in a later chapter.

B. Does God Exist? Being Fooled by a Misdirected Question

Sometimes we fool ourselves by asking the wrong question and then trying to answer it. I got married the summer before my second year of graduate school. When I returned to classes in the fall, a friend and fellow student invited me out for coffee. When we had settled ourselves at the table, he said,

"You're just recently married, so tell me, how do you know when you have met the right person?" I said, "You're kidding, right?" He said, "No, I'm serious. Someday I'd like to be married and have a family, but I don't know how you can tell when you've found the right person." I teasingly responded, "You begin by interviewing as many young women as you can, writing a little note card for each one interviewed. Then when you have interviewed them all, you call back the top ten for a second round of interviews. Then you narrow it to three, and finally down to one." He earnestly responded, "But that's going to take an awful lot of time." Finally, I broke down laughing and pointed out to him that I had given him a stupid answer because he had asked a stupid question. When he asked what was stupid about the question, I tried to explain that love is not the outcome of a sorting process but more like something one is grasped by and a commitment one makes. That's why the number of people in the pool is irrelevant.

He had put himself in a twist by asking the wrong question. He had been led to ask this question, I suppose, by the fact that we sometimes talk about "finding Mr. Right" or "matches made in heaven." Most of the time, fortunately, we get over that way of thinking. But I suppose there are people out there who are turning fifty who are still waiting for "the right one."

Imagine that a couple has been dating for some time when the girl asks, "Do you love me?" To this question she wants a serious answer. But what does a serious answer look like? The question looks like a request for information, information about the young man. But imagine what would happen if, rather than answering yes or no, he were to say, "Give me a minute and I'll check and see." Why is that a stupid response? Because although the question looks like a request for information, it is not. It is an invitation to voice a commitment. There is nothing to "check," no internal love meter we can take a reading of, no specialist we can consult to measure our glandular secretions or brain-wave patterns. Suppose the young man said, "Well, the last time I had it checked my love pressure was two points below normal, but that was two weeks ago so it may have changed." The young woman will not be happy with his response. She didn't want a report; she wanted a sign of affection and commitment. Yet the question "Do you love me?" looks like a request for information. It's definitely an odd question.

Love language seems to be the source of many such confusions. The sung conversation between Tevya and his wife, Golde, in *Fiddler on the Roof* uncovers many such questions with great insight and humor:

Tevya: Do you love me?

Golde: Do I what?

T: Do you love me?

G: You're a fool.

T: I know, but do you love me?

G: For twenty-five years I've washed your clothes, cooked your meals, cleaned your house, given you children, milked the cow. After twenty-five years, why talk of love right now?

T: Golde, the first time I met you was on our wedding day. I was scared.

G: I was shy.

T: I was nervous.

G: So was I.

T: But my father and my mother said we'd learn to love each other, and now I'm asking, Golde, do you love me?

G: I'm your wife.

T: I know . . . But do you love me?

G: For twenty-five years I've lived with him, fought with him, starved with him, twenty-five years my bed is his. If that's not love what is?

T: Then you love me?

G: I suppose I do.

T: And I suppose I love you too.

Both: It doesn't change a thing, but even so, after twenty-five years it's nice to know.

C. Does God Exist? Being Fooled by Grammar

Charles Lutwidge Dodgson, the author we know as Lewis Carroll, was the creator of *Alice in Wonderland, Alice through the Looking Glass,* and other masterpieces of deep silliness. Dodgson was a professor of mathematics and logic at Christ Church College of Oxford University and possessed an uncanny ability to recognize the grammatical ambiguities in the English language. As a consequence, his stories, often assumed to be children's literature, can also be read philosophically as diagnoses and therapies for linguistic maladies. Consider the following exchange from *Alice through the Looking Glass:*

> "I've sent them all!" the King cried in a tone of delight on seeing Alice. "Did you happen to meet any soldiers, my dear, as you came through the wood?"

"Yes, I did," said Alice: "several thousand I should think."

"But I haven't sent the two Messengers. They're both gone to town. Just look along the road and tell me if you see either of them."

"I see nobody on the road," said Alice.

"I only wish I had such eyes," the King remarked in a fretful tone. "To be able to see Nobody! And at that distance too. Why, it's as much as I can do to see real people by this light."

Later one of the messengers arrives.

"Who did you pass on the road?" the King went on.

"Nobody," said the Messenger.

"Quite right," said the King: "this young lady saw him too. So of course Nobody walks slower than you."

"I do my best," the Messenger said in a sullen tone, "I'm sure nobody walks much faster than I do."

"He can't do that," said the King, "or else he'd have been here first."

The King makes the mistake of supposing that "nobody" refers to some person. The sentence "I see nobody on the road" is grammatically identical to "I see a Messenger on the road." But while the latter sentence is about its grammatical object, the Messenger, the former sentence is not.

Imagine someone claiming, "Lobster is better than bratwurst." A second person responds, "Indeed, nothing is better than lobster." To this a Kinglike third person replies, "Oh, I don't agree, I prefer lobster any day." The second sentence looks as if it's grammatically identical to the first one. It looks to be about nothing and looks (grammatically) as if it's making the claim that nothing is better. But, of course, taking the grammar literally in this case leads to a total misunderstanding. The assertion is not about nothing but about how good lobster is.

St. Augustine, a fifth-century Christian bishop of Hippo, was perplexed about time. It seemed to him that the more he thought about it the less he understood it. He wrote: "What then is time? If no one asks me, I know. If I want to explain it to someone who asks, I do not know" (*Confessions*, XI). What's the problem here? Is it that he is ignorant? Is it that he's intellectually lazy? Is it that time is a subject too deep for the human mind to know? Or does the problem reside with the question "What is time?" and with the assumption resident in the question that time is some sort of thing that can (or ought to) be known?

Philosopher O. K. Bouwsma, in his witty essay "The Mystery of Time" (1965), imagines a man who cannot understand how time is measured by clocks. He understands how a meter stick measures a table, and he understands how a water meter measures the flow of water, but he doesn't understand how a clock measures time. The man works himself into a philosophical sweat over his lack of understanding. Bouwsma's point is that here again is a case of misunderstanding caused by taking a feature of grammar and metaphor (that clocks "measure" the "passage" of time) too literally. If the man knows how to tell time and knows the difference between early and late and knows the date on which to celebrate his wedding anniversary, then there isn't anything he doesn't understand about time. As soon as he begins to think of time as some *thing*, some potential *object* of thought, then he becomes hopelessly confused.

D. Does X Exist? The Temptation of the Question

Recently I was rereading W. T. Jones's *The Classical Mind* (1969), the first volume in his well-known *History of Western Philosophy*. In chapter 4, after explaining "Plato's theory of forms," Jones offers the following comment:

> They [Plato's conception of forms] constitute the public world that the Sophists denied and that function at once as the object of the sciences—physical, social and moral—and the objective criteria against which our judgments in these inquiries are evaluated. As the objects of thought, the forms justify thought in looking for objects. Without the forms there would be nothing, in Plato's view, to look for, and every individual would remain forever isolated in the cave of his own subjective states.
>
> But *are* there forms? Do forms such as Plato described them actually exist? (143)

After describing very well what the forms are, how they work, and how we intellectually access them, what sense does it make to ask if they exist? Plato isn't talking about unicorns or left-handed albino spider monkeys. About such things it makes perfectly good sense to question existence. But forms are not physical objects; they are objects of thought. It would make as much sense to ask, "Do ideas exist?" or "Do concepts exist?" or "Do the things mathematicians talk about exist?" To ask such questions is to make what philosophers call a category mistake. It's not unlike the mistake the Duchess makes in *Alice through the Looking Glass* when Alice tells her there is a lack of bread in the pantry. The Duchess asks, "Is a lack larger or smaller than a loaf?"

This is the major criticism Jones brings against Plato's view—that Plato's argument seems much more to assume the forms and to show their explanatory power than it works to establish their existence. But, given the kind of reality the forms are—as objects of thought—that's exactly the kind of argument one would hope for. An argument to establish their existence (as though they were objects in space and time) would be totally inappropriate. Why doesn't Jones see that? Is there a kind of perennial philosophical temptation to assume that reality is exhausted by existing things and that *the question of existence* is always relevant and crucial? If so, perhaps we should identify this perennial temptation as a fallacy and give it an appropriate label to help us avoid it in the future. For the present, let's call it the "but does it exist?" fallacy.

Laws exist—but justice? Yet, justice has reality sufficient to call every existing law to account. There are more or less just laws. Justice is the standard by which laws are judged. Laws come and go, but in an important sense justice is eternal. In some cases, the question of existence is relevant. We may, for example, wish to know whether Ohio has a law against dueling. Does such a law exist? But about justice, the question of existence is inappropriate. Is the same thing true about God?

FROM THE CLASSROOM: STUDENT QUESTIONS & RESPONSES

Q: How can we tell whether a question makes sense? The questions "Does time exist?" and "Do you love me?" and "Does God exist?" seem to make sense. But you claim they don't. How can we tell?

R: We need to ask ourselves, "What are we doing when we say such things?" What we may discover is that we're not doing what we seem to be doing. Sometimes what looks like a question can be used to do something else, but sometimes it's just nonsense.

Q: So, if my girlfriend asks me, "Do you love me?" I'm supposed to critique her question?

R: No, my advice is to buy her some flowers or write her a poem.

Q: I heard my science teacher consider the question "What is the size and shape of space?" Was he asking a nonsense question?

R: I think he probably was. How can one ask spatial questions about space itself? It's sort of like asking, "How long was it before time began?" Suppose a teacher gave you an assignment: "In twenty words (or pages) explain the relationship of language to the world." I hope that you would have the sense to point out that something impossible has been demanded. If the question is wrong, deconstruct the question. Don't add to the confusion by answering it.

Q: Isn't a lot of philosophical thinking like Augustine's puzzling about the nature of time? Would Bouwsma say that an awful lot of philosophical pondering is an attempt to answer unanswerable questions?

R: Yes, I think he would. But I recommend reading further in Bouwsma's essays to see the kinds of questions he would include there. Following the lead of Ludwig Wittgenstein, Bouwsma would say that we discover the meaning of language by seeing how it is used, not by vainly searching for its referent.

Q: How can a thing that doesn't exist transform lives?

R: Be careful how you ask this question. What I'm asserting is that the question "Does God exist?" is faulty. I'm not asserting that the question is good and that the answer is "No." I'm not being an atheist. I'm being skeptical about the question.

But assuming you understand that, I would move on to some other examples: I may hope for something that doesn't exist, and that hope can transform my life. I may fear something that doesn't exist, and that fear may transform my life. Just remember, existence does not exhaust reality.

I think it's improper to say that time exists or space exists, but if you want to see the reality of space and time made dramatically manifest, watch a production of Shakespeare's *Romeo & Juliet*. It's a tragedy that turns around the textures of time and space.

QUESTIONS FOR CRITICAL REFLECTION

1. The claim is made above that the question "How do you find the right woman/man?" is misframed and does not deserve a serious answer. Do you agree, or do you think there is a method someone can use to help in the search for true love? Can you think of other examples of similarly "misframed questions"?

2. There is definitely something odd about the question "Does time exist?" The argument is made here that there is, analogically, something wrong with asking, "Does God exist?" Are the cases analogical? Why? Why not? What kinds of reasons will help us in thinking out an issue like this?

3. Is a cloud a thing or a process? Are we misled by the fact that the word *cloud* is a noun in English? Is it better to focus on *clouding*? The suggestion is made that we are tempted to think about God as a thing (that may or may not exist) because *God* is a noun in English and other European languages. Can you imagine an alternative, for example, as a verb, *godding*, or as an adjective or adverb, *godly*?

4. Pursuing Bouwsma's suggestion further, would it make sense to say that a person understands the term *God* perfectly well if they understand how to *use* the term in contexts of prayer, praise, storytelling, and so forth. For such a person, would theology be worse than useless? Would talk *about* God be a serious mistake?

5. Can you come up with a better name for the temptation philosophers have to ask, "Yes, but does it exist?" Do you agree that it should be identified as a fallacy?

6. The claim is made that existence does not exhaust reality. What other kinds of reality are there? Several decades ago, the American philosopher Paul Weiss wrote a book titled *Modes of Being*. Before looking up his work, see if you can imagine what other modes, besides existence, he might have included.

7. The argument is made here that "I love you" is not a report but a commitment; its meaning is not descriptive but conative. Can you find other examples of language that sound like a report but may function differently?

3. Questioning Assumptions about Religious Language

Assumption 3. Religious Language Is Primarily Referential

Closely connected to the issues raised in chapter 2 about the misleading character of grammar is the assumption that many philosophers have made that language has meaning because it refers to some thing. We learn many terms by having their referents pointed out to us. We may, as children, learn "*ball*" and "*grandpa*" in exactly this way. As students, we may learn in this way how to identify the constellation Orion and the planet Venus as well as how to distinguish a balsam from a spruce. But there are also many terms in our language that we do not learn this way. For example, we learn the meaning of the square root sign without ever looking for its referent; it's a sign that tells us what to do, not what to look for. We may learn to use the word "*gravity*" correctly without ever having its referent pointed out to us. Scientists know perfectly well how to use the term but they also know enough not to set off in search of its referent.

A. Referential and Nonreferential Meaning

In Jonathan Swift's *Gulliver's Travels* (1940), the hero takes great pains to note the languages of the lands he visits. In chapter 5, Gulliver visits the great academy of Lagado, where he encounters professors who are conducting experiments for the improvement of their language and society. Gulliver explains:

> Their first project was to shorten discourse by cutting polysyllables down to one, and leaving out verbs and participles because, in reality, all things imaginable are but nouns.
> The other project was a scheme for entirely abolishing all words whatsoever, and this was urged as a great advantage in point of health as

well as brevity. For it is plain that every word we speak is, in some degree, a diminution of our lungs by corrosion, and, consequently, contributes to the shortening of our lives. An expedient was therefore offered, "that since words are only names for things, it would only be more convenient for men to carry about them such things as were necessary to express a particular business they are to discourse on" (pp. 198–99).

Gulliver explains the disadvantage for people who discourse on many subjects of having to carry many sacks with many objects and the necessity for some of having to hire servants to bear the burden. What no one in the story seems to question are the assumptions made here: that nouns are the primary carriers of meaning and that all nouns mean by referring to some experienceable thing. Most of us know enough to question these assumptions, but it is amazing how frequently they are made.

One way of explaining the mistake made above about time is that it makes the referentialist assumption that time-language is about some thing—time—and that we understand such language only when we are able to clearly conceive what this thing is. But what if time-language is not referential? What if its function is not to talk *about* time nor to refer *to* it but to use it to talk *about events in the world*—just as we might also say that the mistake that is made in misunderstanding "Nothing is better than lobster" is to assume that "nothing"-language refers to nothing rather than its being a way of talking about the goodness of other food.

When we learn, as children, to use God-language in prayer, hymns, stories, and other worship occasions, no one sees the need to indicate the reference of the term. Not even the priest or rabbi or pastor can pull God out of a bag to show us what God-language means. No one points to an object and says the word "*God*" the way they might point to an object in the garden and introduce us to the word "*eggplant*." Why not? One answer is to say that the referent is not present but absent. Another is to claim that the language is meaningless simply because its referent does not exist. That explanation leads us, later on, to wonder whether there is such a referent and to generate arguments pro and con regarding the existence of this referent God.

But another explanation is to say that the lack of the referent for the word "*God*" is not a problem because God-language is not primarily referential. Perhaps God-language functions to focus our attention on the world and life, not on some absent or questionably existent referent. If God-language is not referential, then theology (understood as language *about* God) is a mistake of a very fundamental sort.

B. My Son's Atheism

When my youngest son was eight years old, he announced one day that he no longer believed in God. I asked him why he had come to that conclusion. He said, "Because I've never seen God anywhere." At that point, his grandmother interjected, "You think that at eight years old you're a good judge of what there is in the world?" He said, "Do you mean that I just haven't looked in the right places?" She said, "You haven't looked in heaven." I sat silently, grimaced, and shook my head. Later, I said to my son, "I agree with you more than with your grandma, but I think you're both making a big mistake. Someday I'll try to explain to you the kind of mistake it is."

The assumption my son was making was that God-language functions like much of our language, that is, by referring to an object and then describing the object. This I will call the *referentialist assumption*: that theological language has meaning by referring. One "believes" such language if one thinks there is such a referent in the world. My son had ceased to be a believer in that sense. His grandmother had translocated the referent. She, also making the referentialist assumption, saw theological language as referring to a realm beyond the world, to the "supernatural" or to heaven. What I wanted to do was question the assumption that both were making, namely, that theological language is fundamentally referential.

If God-language is referential, then my son's question is perfectly appropriate. "Where is the referent?" is a good question to ask. But if God-language does not function referentially, then how does it function?

C. How Is God-Language Used?

Some philosophers have argued that religious language performs the function of expressing emotion, somewhat similar to shouting "Hurrah!" at a football game. That sentence does not make any assertion, and therefore when someone says "Hurrah!" we cannot meaningfully ask "True or false?" We cannot critique its claim because it doesn't make any. Some devotees of religion like this account of God-language because it relieves them of having to answer critical questions, that is, demonstrating the truth or meaningfulness of their assertions. But the problem with this defensive posture is that it robs religious language of all cognitive content.

A second approach to religious language is to see it performing a conative function—for example, to see it as a performative statement, such as "I promise to pay this bill by the end of the month." The sentence doesn't describe something. Rather, it *does* something—it makes a commitment. British philosopher Richard Braithwaite argued that the fundamental creedal statements of Christianity actually function to say something like "I commit myself to leading an *agapeistic* form of life" (that is, a life devoted to nonselfish love). I think that Braithwaite is at least partly right. Religious language is a language of life commitment. As we have seen, if such commitment is missing, we have good reason to question whether beliefs are religious at all. But although conative theories have something right, I do not believe they are the whole answer.

A former colleague of mine once showed me the antique microscope he had just purchased. It was made of heavy metal with well-wrought brass knobs and other hardware. It was a century-old model with a reflective mirror and the single eyepiece. "A beautiful old microscope," I said. "What are you planning to look at?" He answered, "Oh, nothing, it's not to be used; it's just to be looked at. It's the microscope that Professor X used when he investigated the cause and cure of Q." I don't remember who he said the owner was or what the disease was; they were not familiar to me. But I do remember being disappointed that this fine tool was not going to be used but would just sit on the shelf being admired.

God-language can be used to focus attention, or it can become the focus of attention. It can be used to think *with*, or it can be thought *about*. In this respect, it is like the example of time we regarded earlier. Time is a vocabulary for talking about the world. As Augustine pointed out, great problems ensue when we turn our attention to thinking and talking *about* what we are perfectly able to think *with*. I think this same thing occurs with God-language. As soon as we turn God into the object of attention, we begin to confuse ourselves as well as others.

How, then, is God-language used? My contention is that this is a different wording of the question that we asked earlier: "How is God's reality manifest?" I discuss below a partial list of such uses or manifestations.

First, the encounter with God is a being-called. Humans are called; their lives are given a focus and meaning, an orientation and purpose. Moses was called to liberate his people. Saul and, later, David were called to be kings of Israel. St. Paul was called to be the communicator of the Christian vision throughout the non-Jewish Mediterranean world. Mother Teresa was called to serve the poorest and most desperate street people in Calcutta. Martin Luther King Jr. was called to a life devoted to racial equality, justice, and human understanding. Calling is one way in which the reality of God is manifest.

But, we might respond, that happens only to a few unique individuals; it doesn't happen to most of us. The Christian reformer Martin Luther would disagree with us about that. Luther argued that all humans have a calling, a vocation. It doesn't necessarily call us to something unusual and extraordinary, as in the above examples. Luther maintained that each of us has some gift and is given some opportunity to serve the needs of those who are our neighbors. In his view, parenting and farming and nursing, fish pickling and street cleaning, being the mayor and being a teacher of third graders, and so forth are all vocations, callings to serve in love the real needs of the world.

Second, the encounter with God is occasion for life transformation. Several of the examples of calling cited above are also cases of profound self-transformation. Persons may become something quite different than they have been. Their plans and strategies may change, but so may their goals and ends. Things that mattered little become their highest value, and things that mattered a great deal now may count for nothing. Many people pray to God that their desires be fulfilled and that their fears be avoided. The God they encounter in such prayers is a tool for their own projects. But imagine truly making a prayer that says, "Thy will be done." There is a hymn whose refrain reads, "Shepherd me, O God, beyond my hopes, beyond my fears, from death into life." When I first read that line in a worship service, it stuck in my throat. I stopped singing and said, to myself, "Who has the courage to pray such a prayer?" To do so would be to invite, or at least to allow, self-transformation.

Third, the encounter with God is a discovery of responsibility. The Genesis creation narrative shows us as humans who, of all the creatures, converse with their creator. In that narrative, humans are told, called, commanded, and brought to account. Being response-able, we also discover we are responsible. The bible is a complex chronicle of this human conversation with God, a conversation where humans are questioned, learn, and are brought to account, and a conversation where God is questioned and brought to account as well. Many psalms express deep questions:

> My God, my God, why have you forsaken me? Why are you so far from helping me, from the sounds of my groaning? (Psalm 22)
>
> How long, O Lord? Will you forget me forever? How long will you hide your face from me? Consider and answer me O Lord, my God. (Psalm 13)

The book of Job is one long calling of God to account. And we learn at the end that Job's relentless questioning is not impious, in spite of being viewed as such by his neighbors.

Fourth, the encounter with God is a thanksgiving. It is a moment of recognizing giftedness, of celebration, and of sharing. Once again, many psalms (as well as a great number of hymns) can be given in evidence:

> The earth is the Lord's and the fullness thereof, the world and those who dwell therein. (Psalm 24)
>
> O taste and see that the Lord is good! (Psalm 34)

Fifth, the encounter with God is an occasion of knowing and self-discovery; it is the opposite of fabrication and phoniness. One cannot lie in the presence of God. If one is lying or putting on airs, the one in whose presence this is done is automatically an idol. Addressing God is the occasion for absolute self-honesty, or self-honesty as absolute as humans can manage:.

> O Lord, you have searched me and known me.
> You know when I sit down and when I rise up,
> You discern my silent thoughts from afar. [Psalm 139]

Sixth, the encounter with God brings with it a new or renewed regard for justice, for respect, for seeing a child of God in the most unlovely of persons. As a friend and former student of mine said:

> When I look at my class of middle schoolers, I am tempted to see kids tossed onto the garbage dump of society. They are poor, they are afraid, they are poorly educated, they are mean, and many are violent. But then I see them as children of God, as persons loved by God, and I go to work on them and go to work for them. I won't give up on them even though most have given up on themselves.

Seventh, the encounter with God is an occasion of hope. The previous quote illustrates that as well.

Eighth, the encounter with God is an encounter with self-transcendence. That is another way of summarizing all the things we've said thus far. A god one can lie to is no God at all. A god one can manipulate is no God at all. A god who is simply a manifestation of my wishes is no God at all. A god from whom we have nothing transforming to learn is no God at all. A god who does not challenge us to risk is no God at all. A malleable, manipulatable, nontransforming reality is an idol, a mere embodiment of my own or the culture's ego.

This is not an exclusive list by any means, but it indicates the kinds of experiences and encounters in which the reality of God is manifest. These experiences, in turn, provide us with a context for understanding how God-language means. It is through such things, not through a search for the God referent, that such language becomes meaningful for the community of faith.

Do religious people think there is one more thing in the room (or the world) than nonreligious people do? Do they take inventory and then add, "Oh yes, and don't forget, there is God." If the referentialist approach is right, then that is what they should do. But if the referentialist approach is a mistake, then the difference is not in the "one more thing" but in the way one regards the world, its contents, and one's self in it. If the referential reading of theological language (language about God) is a mistake, then so is the age-old philosophical enterprise of making and refuting theistic arguments.

FROM THE CLASSROOM: STUDENT QUESTIONS & RESPONSES

Q: In this section you really lost me. How can a word have a meaning if it doesn't have a referent?

R: I probably should have given more examples. Consider the sentence "If it rains, the picnic will be held in the gymnasium." The words *rain*, *picnic*, and *gymnasium* are all referring words; we learn their meaning by having their referents pointed out to us. But consider the words *if . . . then*. We learn those words by seeing not their referents but how they function. They relate the other terms in the sentence in a particular way. It would be silly to go around looking for referents for these words.

Q: Yes, but isn't that because they are not nouns?

R: Good question. Let's try another example, $\sqrt{x}$, or as we'd say it in ordinary English, "the square root of x." The term *square root* is a noun, but it doesn't name an object; rather, it performs a function—that is, it tells us what to do with the quantity that's under the sign. Thus, though it is a noun grammatically, it functions much more as a verb. Better yet is to call it what mathematicians would: a function.

Another example might be the word *health*. It's certainly a noun, but I don't think it refers to any thing. Health is the proper functioning of an organism. We can focus on it only because we recognize the symptoms of the organism when it's not functioning properly. We treat diseases and malfunctions rather than spending our time searching for health. That's why I'm more likely to go to a medical doctor rather than a philosopher when I'm not feeling well. Health is certainly not a useless concept, but it's fairly useless to go in search of its referent.

Education is a noun, but there is no thing that is its referent. The reality is the set of activities we call learning. We mislead ourselves (and others) by saying, "I got an education." It's less misleading to say, "I am practicing the guitar," or "I am reading Proust," or "I am writing a reflective essay every week."

Q: I'm planning to go to seminary when I graduate. Eventually, I'd like to go on to study theology. Are you implying that the study of theology would be a big mistake?

R: If theology is primarily talk *about* God, then I would say you need to examine the referentialist assumption, that is, that God is a something to be talked *about*. But is that the only way of regarding theology? A very renowned theologian, Gordon Kaufman, begins more than one of his books on theology by talking about the breadth and depth of human existence. He believes that theology has to be about humans and the world as well as about God. Or, maybe a better way to put it would be to say that Kaufman's theology is about humans and the world in the light of God. Even the short list of ways that God's reality is manifest in human life shows that there's plenty to be studied. I don't want to discourage your theological studies; I just want to make them more reflective.

QUESTIONS FOR CRITICAL REFLECTION

1. Make a list of words that we learn to use as children that do not have referents. How do we learn them if no one can point out what they refer to?

2. My son's "referentialist assumption" can easily be explained by noting his age at the time. But what accounts for the same assumption on the part of his grandmother? What accounts for it in the many philosophers who have constructed arguments (pro and con) for God's existence?

3. Does a religious person believe there is another thing in the room (or in the world) than a nonreligious person does? If that is not the right way to talk about the difference between them, then what is a better way?

4. This chapter offers several examples of ways in which the reality of God is manifest. Are there important manifestations that have been left off this list? Is there a deep pattern in this list? What, if anything, can we learn from it about the proper use of God-language?

Part Two

Rethinking the Philosophy of Religion

4. Rethinking Religious Faith

In part 1, we considered three assumptions that seem basic to philosophy of religion as it is usually pursued. The assumptions are that (1) belief is the focal act of faith, (2) God's existence is the focal belief, and (3) God-language is referential—that is, it gets its meaning by referring to a being, God, whose existence is in question. We have also collected a number of reasons why each of these assumptions should be questioned.

At this point, an acute reader will ask, "If belief is not focal to faith, then what is?" and "If religious language is not to be understood referentially, then how should it be understood?" These questions are addressed in this chapter.

Religion as a Way of Seeing

Rabbi Harold Kushner, in his book *Who Needs God* (1989), writes this provocative remark: "Religion is not primarily a something to be believed. . . . Religion is first and foremost a way of seeing" (27). What is the difference in these two approaches? What does it mean to approach something as "a something to be believed" as contrasted to something that informs a way of seeing?

We can read the Genesis creation narrative as "a something to be believed," and we can then either believe it or not. But we can also read it as a different kind of text, namely, as one that informs our vision of the world (as extravagant and wondrous gift) and of ourselves (as creatures given a particular role as response-able and responsible stewards of the creation and as beings who are tempted to be the owner and master thereof). If we read it as a something to be believed, it is primarily a text about what happened in the past. If we read it as informing a way of seeing, then it is as much about the present and the future as it is about the past. The former way of reading addresses the theoretical question "How did things get started?" The latter way of reading primarily addresses the questions "What kind of world is this?" "How are we to be in it?"

The psalmist inhabits a world shaped by such a seeing:

The earth is the Lord's and the fullness thereof,
The world and those who dwell therein. (Ps. 24:1)

O taste and see that the Lord is good. (Ps. 34:8)

We can read the Christmas narrative in the Gospel of Luke. Once again, it may be read primarily as a something to be believed. If we confront it that way, certain questions push themselves into the foreground: Can virgins give birth? Was there a census and a taxing that required a peasant family to travel from Nazareth to Bethlehem at this time? Did Herod order a mass murdering of male infants shortly thereafter? Is it credible that this peasant family could have fled to Egypt and only later returned to Nazareth? Are angels physical beings? If not, how do they speak and sing? What eyewitness to these events related them to Luke? Why didn't the other Gospels bother to recount these amazing events? What functions did miraculous (and virginal) birth narratives play in the ancient world?

If we read the story as informing a way of seeing, none of these questions hold anything more than a passing curiosity. Instead, a whole new agenda of questions presents itself: Is the King of Kings and Lord of Lords, the eternal Logos, really to be found in something so humble? A tiny village? A stable? A Jewish peasant family? An infant in rags born in a stable? Can something so cosmic be embodied in something so powerless? Is there a truth that shepherds might have revealed to them that imperial governors would not? As a consequence of this story, how do I regard shepherds? How do I regard imperial governors? Once again, this seeing is much more about how things *are*, not just about how they *were*. A sight- and life-informing story is more about the future and present than it is about the past.

Consider the following poem, which came to me in a Christmas letter:

You Took Me by the Hand—Christmas Poem 2007

You took me by the hand
And steered me to this alien town,
To see these humans busy with their daily tasks,
Finding food, keeping warm, avoiding the authorities, bearing a child,

Working, trudging home, trying to make it again today.
A homely, random, apparently hopeless place, this town,
Like so many we pass by
Not deserving a pause or a photo post-card.

You took me by the eye
Just to catch the noteless side of this nowhere
Which has the character of everywhere un-noticed.
These people are nobody to me. Peasants and poor locals,
Maybe he's the local law, she's definitely the waitress.
Some soldiers hang together smoking further down the way.
Why stop here? What's to see? Plain folks? Travelers?
A woman huddled shivering in the back booth of the diner,
Her newborn wrapped in a stained dish towel?
Her man trying to scrounge enough to buy two pancakes and some milk
    at the counter?

You took me by the mind
And pushed me through the diner door
And said, "King of Kings, Lord of Lords, Child of God,
Light of the World?" And I said, "No way. Get serious.
I saw the emperor once in a parade, and the generals.
I know the governor, I have a friend who's his lieutenant,
The bishop even knows my name, I think.
But nobody here even has a name, less chance a title,
Unless it would be 'the least of these.'"

You took me by the heart
And slapped me around 'til dizzy, displaced, bumping into things
I fell on my knees.
"What if . . . " you asked, "the most important thing is the least
    important,
The smallest is the greatest, the littlest detail is cosmic, the biggest deal
    is comic?
What if the heavenly choir squawks over the kitchen radio?
If the wise men are all truckers from Toledo?
What if the emperor has no clothes and the king has a bare butt?"

"I wasn't born yesterday, you know," I objected.
"Oh yeah? Then how about today?" you replied.

Anonymous

Here, the Christmas narrative in Luke informs the poet's way of seeing a small-town truck stop. Bethlehem is not just some town far away in a time long ago in a land never visited; it is the place the poet is. The story in Luke has transformed this world, not primarily affirmed another one. I may have memorized the narrative (e.g., Luke's Christmas story) and still have missed having it speak to me in a way that informs the way I see and hear and respond to everything else in the world. Can I stop for coffee on my way home after a Christmas Eve service and not see in a different way the poor couple with the newborn who are in the back booth of the diner?

Buddhist teacher Thich Nhat Hanh, in his book *Old Path, White Clouds: Walking in the Footsteps of the Buddha* (1991), relates an encounter between Gautama Siddhartha and an untouchable who was hauling a double load of human excrement to be dumped. The untouchable saw the master coming along the street with his disciples. To avoid making contact, the untouchable put down his load and fled, walking out into the river to avoid the master. The master turned from his path, went to the water's edge, and addressed the untouchable:

"My friend, please come closer so that we might talk."

"Lord, I don't dare!"

"Why not?" asked the Buddha.

"I am an untouchable. I don't want to pollute you and your monks."

The Buddha replied, "On our path we no longer distinguish between castes. You are a human being like the rest of us. We are not afraid we will be polluted. Only greed, hatred and delusion can pollute us. . . . What is your name?"

"My Lord, my name is Sunita."

"Would you like to become a bhikku like the rest of us?"

"I couldn't."

"Why not?"

"I'm an untouchable!"

"Sunita, I have already explained that on our path there is no caste. In the Way of Awakening caste no longer exists. It is like the Ganga, Yamuno, Aciravati, Sarabhu, Mahi, and Rohini rivers. Once they empty into the sea, they no longer retain their separate identities. A person who leaves home to follow the Way leaves caste behind whether he is brahman, ksatriya, vaisya, sudra or untouchable. Sunita, if you like you can become a bikkhu like the rest of us."

"No one has ever spoken to me so kindly before. This is the happiest day of my life. If you accept me as your disciple, I vow to devote all my being to practicing your teaching."

"Sariputta! Help me bathe Sunita and bring him a robe. We will ordain him a Bhikku right here on the bank of the river." (279–81)

The interesting thing is that all three of these stories (the Genesis creation story, Jesus' birth story, and the story of Sunita's calling) can function to inform our understanding of the world, of other persons, and of our own character without being believed in the first sense. I may be transformed by one of the stories that Jesus tells or by one of the dialogues that Plato writes about Socrates, without any concern for whether the story is true. It is the Socrates who Plato writes about who inspires me. It is the Buddha whom Nhat Hanh so vividly pictures from whom I learn. It is the Jesus of Mark's Gospel who opens my eyes. In all three of these cases, the historical Socrates, the historical Buddha, and the historical Jesus are of very secondary interest. Even avowed works of fiction can inform our vision of life, personhood, and the world without our once forgetting that they are works of fiction.

One could read Joyce Cary's novel *The Horse's Mouth* (1944) as a something to be believed. Were we to do so, we would want to pursue certain questions: Was there really a British artist named Gulley Jimson? Did he live in a rundown leaky houseboat on the Thames? Was he in constant trouble with the law? Did he and his works finally get recognized as a national treasure at the same time as he was living in poverty in the shadow of the institution that honored him?

Or one could read the novel as a vision-shaping story. In this case, the questions change: Is it possible to have one's eyes opened, one's senses awakened, to the awesome character of the world? Do most of us go through life in a sleep-walking state, barely aware of the world around us? Why does that seem to be so? Why would humans choose such a life? Is being an artist a noble calling, one worthy of emulation and honor, or is it a psychological malady to be avoided, if possible, at all costs?

One can read the Exodus narrative from the Hebrew Scriptures as a something to be believed. Were we to do that, we would focus on certain questions: Is there any historical evidence to suggest that the ancestors of the Hebrew people were, as a nation, slaves in Egypt while Ramses was Pharaoh? Is there evidence of a series of plagues visited on the Egyptians at this time? Did Ramses die from drowning while attempting to cross the Red Sea in his chariot? Was there someone named Moses who, being of Hebrew birth, was raised as part of the royal family of Egypt? Did the Hebrew people wander for forty years in the wilderness before they were led into the "promised land" of Canaan?

Were we to read the same narrative as a vision-shaping story, we would focus on other questions: How does having been a slave shape one's view of slavery? Or one's view of being an oppressed minority? If this is our story, can we then turn around and enslave or oppress others? How does a story that plays out over many generations shape the way one regards the sufferings of the present generation? Can one sustain hope in the presence of calamity? How should a particular place, a "promised land," be part of one's identity as a people?

Quite a few texts (and here I include films, poems, and plays, as well as novels and stories written and acted as well as told) truly have the power to shape and to change one's life. It is interesting to ask someone what kinds of texts have had that life-reorienting power. On my list would be several of the parables of Jesus, Dostoevsky's *Notes from Underground* as well as his *Brothers Karamazov* and *The Idiot*, Joyce Cary's *The Horse's Mouth*, Twain's *Huckleberry Finn*, Plato's dialogues but especially *The Symposium*, and Bergmann's films, including *The Silence, Winter Light, Wild Strawberries*, and his masterpiece, *Fanny & Alexander*. There are others, too, but these are some of the texts that have made me who I am.

I just finished teaching two sections of a pilot first-year seminar. In that class, we read one novel, half a dozen short stories, and several essays, and watched two films. I encouraged students to encounter the texts so that eventually they could get to the level of asking, "What does this text mean to me?" "What relevance does it have for my life or my career as a student?" "In what way is the reading of this life shaping?" Toward the end of the class, one of the students asked me, "Where else in the curriculum can one find classes like this, classes focused on reading literature for its human meaning? I've looked through the catalog but haven't found any courses where texts are read with such purposes in mind." I admitted to the student that he was probably right. Where do we read novels, stories, and films as literature? Unfortunately, often even in literature classes we read texts because they are embodiments of some literary movement or theory, not because we believe that the reader will grow significantly through the encounter. So I thought about relabeling some of my classes. Perhaps now I'll call them "Texts That Will Give You a

Whack in the Head," or "Films That Will Grab Your Ass," or "Mind-Opening Stories." But please remember that none of these texts needs to be believed to have this effect. They affect us while we are completely aware that they are fictions. The texts need only to affect our way of seeing—ourselves, others, and the world.

I am not claiming that the Genesis narrative and the Christmas narrative and the Buddha narrative cited above have to be regarded as works of fiction. I am claiming that whether they are or not fiction isn't the question that preoccupies us if we can engage these stories as a way of seeing, as stories that potentially change our world and change the self that sees. They have a world-transforming and self-transforming power. They are literature in the full sense of the word. As Northrop Frye wrote in *The Educated Imagination* (2002), "You wouldn't go to *Macbeth* to learn about the history of Scotland. You'd go to it to learn what a man feels like after he has gained the whole world and lost his soul" (64).

I know that some people lose all interest in stories if they are not true in the "something to be believed" sense. I simply don't understand that point of view. As a historian, I might be interested in what the Gospel of Luke tells me about the reign of Herod. But I don't see anyone being particularly interested in its historicity *as a religious concern*. The religious concern seems to me to be how this story, whether historical or not, might inform and indeed transform how everything else is seen. The fact that a story, like the parables Jesus tells in the Gospels, has the power to change our view of reality including ourselves—now *that* is interesting.

Religious Language as Parable?

British philosopher Austin Farrar argued that theological sentences are best understood as parables. He stated: "Because the primary subject of theological statements is, according to unbelievers, preposterous and according to believers 'transcendent', the statements about Him cannot be anything but parables borrowed from the world of our direct acquaintance" (Farrar, 1957, 10). But what does it mean for something to be a parable? The word "*parable*" comes from a Greek root that means "to compare." Many dictionaries define *parable* as a brief, homely, and usually fictitious story that teaches a moral or religious lesson. John Dominic Crossan, in his provocative little book *The Dark Interval: The Theology of Story* (1975), talks about parable as a story that subverts both our typical answers and our questions. It is a story that turns the customary world upside down and leaves us with a shocking new way of seeing.

Farrar thinks of parable as a statement with a double referent: " 'That to which the parables are applied' is, indeed, an ambiguous phrase. In one sense the parables are applied to God and to his actions. But in another sense the whole parabolic discourse about God and his actions is applied to 'life' " (Farrar, 1957, 12).

Farrar goes on to develop the example of what he calls moral regard for humans. It is by way of understanding God as creator and redeemer that we come to regard our neighbor as human in the moral sense, that is, as deserving moral regard. Farrar writes: "The worth of the man is determined by his place in God's purpose, and it is not a worth that in any way hides or palliates his imperfections" (20). Our understanding of God (as creator and redeemer) therefore shapes our experience of the man. But the reverse is also true. Farrar states: "It is not in some fabulous world beside the human that God is recognized or honored, but in the friend. . . . God the creator of the man is seen and regarded in the man" (23). Theological language is parabolic insofar as it reshapes the experienced world by means of another vocabulary. From that point on, the two references shape and give meaning to each other.

We come to see a person in a particular way because of the creation and redemption stories. But we also, Farrar would argue, come to understand the talk about God because we see what moral regard of one human for another is like. An exclusive attention to the God referent makes us miss what the story illumines, namely, our lives. An exclusive attention to the latter, however, leaves us with a life that's missing a dimension: in Farrar's example, the moral dimension.

Poetry: A Prerequisite for Faith?

Part of theologian Karl Rahner's lifelong work, *Theological Investigations* (1979), is a short essay titled "Poetry and the Christian." There, Rahner poses the question of whether there is a preparation that a person must undergo to be or become a Christian. He suggests that there is such a preparation and that it is "a receptive capacity for the poetic word" (357). He explains:

> The first requisite for man's hearing the word of the gospel without misunderstanding it is that his ears should be open for the word through which the silent mystery is present. . . . Christianity needs such words, it needs practice in learning to hear such words. For all its words would be misunderstood, if they were not heard as words of the mystery, as the coming of the blessed, gripping, incomprehensibility of the holy (358, 359)
>
> The second requisite . . . is the power to hear words that reach the heart. . . . [Such words] are sacral, even sacramental; they help to effect what they signify and penetrate creatively into the primordial centre of man. (360)
>
> The third requisite . . . is the power of hearing the word that unites. Words distinguish but the words which call to the all-pervading mystery and reach the heart, are words which unite. . . . They make the whole present in the one; they speak of one death and we taste the death of all; they voice one joy and joy itself penetrates our heart; they tell of one man and we have learned to know something of all men. (360, 361)
>
> The fourth requisite . . . is the power of recognizing the inexpressible mystery in the word . . . the power of becoming aware of the incarnational . . . of hearing the Word become flesh. (361)

Toward the end of his essay, Rahner engages the question of whether everything that calls itself Christian really is such, and he is willing to admit that this is not so. He is also willing to admit that Christianity and poetry are not the same thing. But having said that, he continues:

> But really great Christianity and really great poetry have an inner kinship. . . . Great poetry exists only where man radically faces what he is. . . . Apart from having confident faith there is practically only one thing we can do here: it is to ask ourselves how far we have become men. One way . . . of knowing this is to see whether our ears are opened to hear with love the word of poetry. (367)

If we do not have such ears, how does the Christian message sound to us? How does the poetry of humankind sound?

What is this gift that the person opened to the world of poetry has? What is the gift that enables the transformation of seeing mentioned earlier by Kushner? My candidate for this capacity is human imagination.

Faith and Imagination

Ways of seeing are shaped by imagination, as are ways of being. Picture five different people walking through the same woodland acreage: a lumberer, a realtor, a zoologist, a nature photographer, and a druid. Each experiences the woods in different ways. Each attends to different things. The lumberer completes the circuit with an estimate of board-feet of lumber and makes a bid on the property with that figure in mind. The realtor sees its potential for residential development and envisions it laid out in homestead plots with little houses on each. The zoologist sees it as habitat for a variety of animal life. The photographer sees it framed by the lens of a camera and notices its pictorial potential. The druid sees it as a sacred place, perhaps inhabited by nature spirits worthy of worship. Although the woods they see may be physically the same acreage, there is a sense in which they inhabit very different worlds. Their ways of seeing in most cases imply different ways of being human.

For the purposes of this illustration, I have assumed these five people are different persons. But they need not be. For example, the realtor may turn into a nature photographer on the weekend. Some ways of seeing we can "put on" and "take off." I may, for a brief period, be able to think of my children (or myself for that matter) as exemplars of statistics. But if I begin to regard them or all people in that way, then I have become quite a different person living in quite a different world. If I begin to think of all my relationships as economic ones, then not only do I know how to use economics as a way of looking at things but I have *become* an economist and the world *is* the sum of economic relations. A friend of mine who is an attorney commutes from Manhattan to Connecticut daily by train. When I told him that I thought that an hour commute would be a great pain, he said, "No, it's good and necessary. It takes me that long to take off my attorney face and put on my family face. A martini is the solvent that helps the mask come off. Without that ritual, I would see everyone as clients or adversaries. That way of seeing is completely inappropriate for an evening with my family."

Religious Faith: An Imagination-Shaped Way of Seeing

Following Rabbi Kushner's provocative suggestion and informed by many examples of different human ways of seeing, I would define religion as *a deep, pervasive, imagination-shaped way of seeing that informs the world and the self that is in it. Faith is continuing intercourse with the sustaining stories, images, and practices that inform such seeing/being.* Faith is imagining, and the seeing (and understanding and living) that flows from it.

I can hear someone responding, "Faith is imagining? What a ridiculous theory. I expected a theory that would take faith seriously, not reduce it to a mere imagining." I am not surprised by this response, but what I hope to show is that there is nothing *mere* about imagining and that to connect something with imagination is not to demean it or to decrease its importance.

Some Prejudices against Imagination

We often suppose that imagination is opposed to reality. A child with a vivid imagination may spend her time in a make-believe world. One can suppose that her parents at some point will say to such a child, "It's now time you left your imaginary world behind and learned to live in the real world."

We frequently equate the idea of imagination with fantasy, dreaming, and wishful thinking. We suppose that the imaginative is equivalent to the imaginary. What we often fail to recognize is that there are many cases when knowing the real world requires a vivid imagination. Imagination is not just a "seeing what is not there"; in many cases, it is *how we see what is there.* Without imagination, many of the ways we have of knowing would not get off the ground. The best way to appreciate the role of imagination is to consider some examples.

Imagination Example: Architect

An architect sees a building as a floor plan or as a section, but he does not actually *see* the building that way for it would require him to be in a position he cannot achieve, somehow hanging in midair above the floor of a building that has floors but no ceilings. The floor plan or section he draws requires an act of imagination, a projection of a view he cannot in real life achieve. That view, that combination of seeing and not seeing, ends up informing his actual view. He ends up seeing the actual building from the point of view of the imagined one so he can explain to the client, for example, "And your new kitchen will begin right here and extend out beyond this wall another ten feet." An architect who could not imagine a floor plan or a section would be severely limited; in fact, I doubt he could be an architect at all. The knowledge of the architect is imagination-informed experience.

Imagination Example: Astronomer

A scientist considers the paths of the planets around the sun and explains their relative size, position, and motion, and how their mass influences the orbits of each. In order to do this, she must sketch a view of the solar system from a point of view that no human has ever physically achieved. This scientific view is not imaginary in the fantasy sense, yet it requires great imagination as well as careful calculation in order to get it right. Very similar things happen when scientists construct models of the atom or predict the weather or try to model the consequences of global warming. Imagination, in such cases, is not a flight from reality but a necessary move in the knowing of reality. One cannot see the real relations of sun and planets without a serious exercise of imagination. Many of the crucial moves in the history of science occurred when scientists learned to see the world in a different way as the consequence of a re-imagining.

Imagination Example: Isaac Newton

Every high school kid knows that Isaac Newton discovered gravity. They're also likely to know that gravity is part of every phenomenon we experience. Gravity keeps the cereal and milk in the bowl, it keeps us from floating around the room, it keeps the car on the road, and so forth. If gravity is part of every phenomenon we experience, then why did it take until the end of the seventeenth century for some scientist to "discover" it? How could wise persons of the past have missed the presence of such an omnipresent thing? They were able to do this because gravity is not a thing to be seen so much as it is a way of seeing everything.

Newton's discovery required that he look at nature in a way different from how his predecessors did. Newton looked at the moon and asked, "Why does it move in a (more or less) circular path around the earth? Why doesn't it fly off in a straight line into the depths of space?" It had never occurred to anyone before Newton to ask such a far-fetched question, to say nothing of answering it, because everyone had assumed that the circular motion of the moon was natural—that is, that it required no explanation. It was simply in the nature of the moon to do this, just as it's natural for Italians to wave their hands when they talk. The answer "because he's Italian" explains the latter. So, for millennia, "because it's the moon" was the accepted answer.

Newton's first law of motion asserts that an object in motion will remain in motion in a straight line unless it is perturbed by some outside influence.

But look around. Where is there an object that does this? The motion of stones and bowling balls is not eternal nor is it straight line. The movement of planets or the moon may seem eternal, but it's not straight-line motion either. Newton makes eternal straight-line motion the very premise of his system. Yet, an object that actually behaves as so described is a complete fiction. Why? Because the motion of every object is "perturbed." What is this perturbation that influences the motion of everything in the universe? Gravity.

Newton's discovery was not to find some hidden thing. It was to look at the world in a different way, a way shaped by the hypothesis that normal motion was straight-line constant motion and that any other kind of motion needed to be explained. The moon does not move in a straight line; therefore, there must be some outside force sufficient to bend its path.

Many of Newton's scientific contemporaries thought he had lost his mind. "Prove to us that straight-line constant motion is the norm. Show us where in nature such motion occurs," they demanded. He could not. "Show us this force that you call gravity; it sounds like an occult explanation to us," they challenged. He could not show it except by pointing at everything. "Explain to us how the mass of the earth affects the motion of the moon at such a distance. Where's the cord? What's the mechanism of it?" they persisted. Newton had no answer.

The point of going on about the example of Newton is for you to notice what a weird view Newton had proposed and how legitimate were the concerns of his contemporaries. Newton's discovery was a new way to see every case of motion in the universe. Straight-line eternal motion as the paradigm changed the way everything was viewed. The "proof" of Newton's vision was what scientists could go on to see as a consequence.

Newton's discovery required an astounding act of re-imagination and re-visioning. In his case, and in the case of many other scientific discoveries (e.g., Lister, Mendeleyev, Maxwell, Einstein), seeing truly and imagining were not opposed to each other. Instead, the former depended on the latter. Scientific knowledge was seeing informed by imagining. That's not all science is, of course, but imagining has proven to be a necessary move that must be made before the careful measuring and testing that science requires can be done.

Imagination Example: Founders of the Democracy

When the founders of the United States were drafting the Declaration of Independence, the Constitution, and the Bill of Rights, they stated that we are all created equal and that we are endowed with certain inalienable rights. There is no way, by looking at real people in the real world, that such claims can be confirmed. We are, in fact, unequal in almost every way—in strength, intelligence, talent, wealth, good looks, and so forth. How, then, could they make such claims, and why would anyone in their right mind believe them?

What they were uttering was not a truth gathered from observation but a truth that changed the way we view humans and their differences. They were saying, "Those differences are there but they should not count for anything, ethically or politically. Politically and legally, justice is blind." The ability to see (and to be blind to seeing) required a particular kind of imagination, just as in the case of the architect and of Newton. The signers of those founding documents had to see certain things that not everyone had seen (equality and human rights) and to be able to see through or see past a lot of things that others were so focused on (race, class, wealth, gender). Just so, the architect has to see the pattern and arrangement of the floor while seeing past ceilings and walls that most of us are impeded by seeing.

Imagination Example: Geometrics

A fairly common definition of the equator is "an imaginary line around the earth equidistant from the poles." Anyone who looks at a map or globe will see that it is covered with a whole bunch of imaginary lines: latitudes, longitudes, polar circles, and so forth. These define the hemispheres and the tropics. They aid in navigation, global positioning, and other processes. Yet, we teach about such "imaginary lines" in school just as if they were important realities, matters of fact rather than mere matters of imagination. I wonder if any parent has ever objected to having such imaginings taught to his gullible son or daughter?

How about the other lines on our maps, those that chart national and state boundaries? A historical atlas will show how many times the boundaries of countries have changed, only later to be changed back again, or how suddenly three countries will appear where previously there was only one. Are these lines realities or imaginings? What we should notice is that the question assumes that these two options are the only ones we have and that they are exclusive. In some ways, national boundaries are artificial, temporary political fictions, as are the nations they mark. But in another domain, these are important realities—realities some people are willing to kill and die over.

The point of all of these examples has been to show that imagination is a necessary ingredient in many kinds of seeing and knowing. We ought to become aware of our tendency to reject things simply because they require a movement of imagination in order to be known or seen or understood. If we have a prejudice against imagination, it is because we mistake imagination for fantasy. We would do well, instead, to value it for the powerful and necessary epistemological tool that it is.

The Power of Imagination: Some Testimonials

Because we seem to be so naturally inclined to devalue imagination, it may help to hear some voices that attest to the power and importance of imagination.

American theologian H. Richard Niebuhr, in his book *The Responsible Self* (1963), wrote:

> We are far more image-making and image-using creatures than we usually think we are, further . . . our processes of perception and conception, of organizing and understanding the signs that come to us in our dialogue with the circumambient world, are guided and formed by images in our own minds. (151, 152)

British philosopher Mary Warnock offers the following description of imagination:

> [Imagination is] a power in the human mind which is at work in our everyday perception of the world, and is also at work in our thoughts about what is absent, which enables us to see the world, whether absent or present, as significant, and also to present this vision to others, for them to share or reject." (Warnock, 1976, 198)

And Craig Dykstra, in *Vision and Character* (1981), writes: "The transformation of the moral life, the transformation of character, is a transformation of the imagination. . . . The function of revelation is to provide us with images by which to see truthfully and realistically" (78, 79).

Garrett Green, in his book *Imagining God* (1989), quotes philosopher John Wisdom: "It seems to me that some belief as to what the world is like is of the essence of religion." Green continues:

> [This] definition is formally functional, taking religion to be something humans do and identifying its essence with the functional aim of that

activity. The material aspect of the definition is provided by the paradigmatic imagination. . . . Put more simply, the function of religious imagination is to tell us "what the world is like" in its broadest and deepest sense. . . . Religions employ that ability in the service of cosmic orientation." (79)

Religion as paradigmatic imagination changes our view of what the world is like. That is a very clear statement of the point the analogy with Newton and Jefferson intended. If God is a paradigm (shaping our attention) rather than an object of attention, then an exclusive attention to God can become a temptation. Martin Buber, in section 3 of his classic *I and You*, writes:

> The meeting with God does not come to a person in order that he or she may thereafter be preoccupied with God, but in order to demonstrate the meaning of the encounter in action in the world. All revelation is calling and sending. But again and again a person may avoid action and turn back to focus on the revealer. This person would rather focus on God than face the world. . . . Just as an ego-maniac does not feel or perceive anything directly but mediates everything through the I that perceives or feels . . . so the theo-maniac . . . will not put the gift into action but focuses exclusively on the giver and consequently misses the meaning of both.

Religious Imagination

The feature film *Gandhi* pictures very clearly the religious situation in India before that country became independent in 1947. Both the Hindu majority and the Muslim minority had wanted the British out and were united in their efforts to achieve this. But neither religious group trusted the other to look after its interests in a post-British India. For the most radically devout Muslims, to be Muslim was to be anti-Hindu; for the most radically devout Hindus, to be a Hindu was to be anti-Muslim. Each religion was informed by a kind of religious chauvinism, an "us versus them" way of looking at the world.

In the midst of this volatile situation stood Mohandas Gandhi, a man who had earned the deep respect of all Indian citizens for his decades-long nonviolent campaign against British colonial occupation and control. But, in spite of this respect, Gandhi perplexed many on both sides of the conflict because he claimed to be both Hindu and Muslim and claimed "brotherhood" not only with Hindus and Muslims but with Christians, Jews, and Sikhs as well. He said that all of these people were "children of God" and should be treated as brothers and sisters. He refused to participate in any conflict of one religion with another and refused to recognize the partition of the country into a Muslim Pakistan and a Hindu India. Gandhi was finally assassinated by a group of Hindu extremists on the eve of his going to pay a visit to "his brothers in Pakistan."

What we see here is the conflict between two very different religious visions. The one religious identity ended up fueling chauvinism and, finally, violence. The other religious vision ended up embracing the "other" by refusing to see otherness as the defining issue, and worked for mutual understanding and peace. It's important to see both as manifestations of religion, both as a way of seeing, both informed by slightly different stories, images, and rituals. But despite the fact that both Gandhi and those who assassinated him claimed the name "Hindu," it is hard to see them as being the same faith at all. This is why I prefer to see religion as the deep, pervasive way of seeing that shapes our world and ourselves. Two people may call themselves by different religious names and still share a view of the world and of themselves. Two people may use the same religious name and still have radically different ways of seeing and being in the world.

About a dozen years ago, I heard a story on National Public Radio about a town that had arrested several homeless people who had taken shelter for the night in the stable of a church's Nativity scene. Many in the congregation and the town, including the pastor or priest, saw their presence as a "desecration." A few in that Christian community, I hope, saw the awesome irony of what had taken place. If so, it is yet another example of how people within a religious tradition may have shockingly different ways of seeing the world.

Perhaps the most important question to ask about a religion is "What vision of the world, the self, and other persons does it engender?" This is the crucial question, it seems to me, whether I am meeting a person from a religion I have never before encountered or if I am encountering a devotee of a religion with which I am quite familiar. Rather than focusing on what the identifying religious name is ("I am a Hindu," "I am a Muslim," "I am a Buddhist," "I am a Sikh") or identifying what the informing story or image is (Jesus on the cross, the elephant-god Ganesh, the meditating Buddha), I will want to know "Who are 'the others' and how do you regard and treat them?" "What kind of place is the natural world and how do you treat it?" "What does it mean to be a person and how does one realize personhood?" "What is good? What, if anything, is evil?" and so forth.

Religious Faith as Experiencing-As

John Hick, contemporary British philosopher, developed an account of faith that is very consistent with the suggestion Kushner made that religion is primarily a way of seeing. Hick's account, published in 1969, predates Kushner's by several decades. Hick begins by noting a great contrast:

> We cognize things that are present before us, this being called perception; and we also cognize things in their absence, this being a matter of holding beliefs about them. And the astonishing fact is that while our religious literature—the Bible, and prayers, hymns, sermons, devotional meditations and so on—confidently presuppose a cognition of God by acquaintance, our theological literature in contrast recognises for the most part only cognition in absence. That is to say, whereas the Bible itself, and other writings directly expressing the life of faith, are full of men's encounters with God . . . the dominant systems of Christian theology nevertheless treat faith as belief, as a propositional attitude. . . . Thus faith, instead of being seen as a religious response to God's redemptive action in the life of Jesus of Nazareth, has been seen instead as primarily an assent to theological truths. . . . Instead of assimilating faith to propositional belief . . . we must assimilate it to perception. I therefore want to explore the possibility that the cognition of God is more like perceiving something . . . than it is like believing a statement about an absent object. (Hick, 1969, 20, 21)

Hick goes on to talk about examples of seeing-as: the duck that can also be seen as a rabbit; the stairway that can be seen as ascending or descending; a bunch of random marks that can finally be seen as a picture of a dog; the beautiful young woman with a large hat who can be seen as the face of a hag. Hick's intention is to show how, for example, the faith of the Hebrew prophets was a way of experiencing the historical events of their day as the self-revealing acts of God. It was their task to share this vision (this way of experiencing) with their contemporaries. Hick writes:

> The Old Testament prophets were vividly conscious of Jahweh as acting in relation to the people of Israel. . . . Through the writings which recall their words and deeds we feel their overwhelmingly vivid consciousness of God

as actively present in their contemporary history.... Humanly explicable events were experienced as acts of God, embodying his wrath or his mercy or his calling the Jewish nation into covenant with him. (31)

Hick argues that experiencing-as is not the oddity that we might suppose it is. In fact, Hick maintains, all experiencing is a kind of experiencing-as. Every time we identify a thing (or misidentify it), we are making an interpretation that requires an experiencing as. We see a fork on a table and, because we have the cultural background and history that we do, we correctly experience it as a fork. But someone from a different culture or a different historical period might not make this identification because "fork" is not an interpretive category that person has. My mother told the story of two neighbors in northern Minnesota, one from Germany and the other from Italy. The latter refused the meal offered by the former on the grounds that "the cabbage had gone bad." The Italian had obviously never heard of sauerkraut and was ready to throw it in the garbage.

Hick goes on to explain that the faith of the early Christian disciples was "the experience of being in the presence of God." Hick writes:

> The primary instance of faith ... consisted in seeing Jesus as the Christ. ... Their experience of following Jesus was also an experience of being in the presence of God's personal purpose and claim and love.... [The] primary response of the first disciples to Jesus as Lord and Christ was not a theory about him which they adopted, but an experience out of which Christian language and theory later grew. (32)

Hick concludes his essay with a discussion of revelation and miracle and sacrament. Revelation is simply the correlative of faith as experience. To the experience of faith, the world is the revelation and God is self-revealingly active in the world and in the life of the perceiver. Miracle, Hick explains, "is an event through which we become vividly and immediately conscious of God as acting towards us" (34). A sacrament, Hick explains, "has the same religious quality as a miracle but differs from other miracles in that it occurs within a liturgical context and is a product of a ritual" (35).

A Critical View and a Response

To this point, we have considered the work of several thinkers who have supported the role of faith as seeing, imagination, and experiencing-as. We should also consider a thinker who addresses such a possibility but regards it critically. The critical view we will consider is one voiced in the 1950s by British philosopher I. M. Crombie in his essay "The Possibility of Theological Statements" (1957). Crombie begins by stating:

> Christianity, as a human activity, involves much more than simply believing certain propositions about matters of fact, such as that there is a God, that He created the world, that He is our judge. But it does involve believing these things, and this believing is, in a sense fundamental; not that it matters more than the other things a Christian does, but that it is presupposed in the other things. (31)

He continues:

> Believing in is logically subsequent to believing that. I cannot believe in Dr. Jones if I do not believe that there is such a person. . . . There are then certain factual beliefs which are fundamental to Christianity. . . . The expression of such beliefs I shall refer to as the making of theological statements. (32–33)

Interestingly, Crombie goes on to spend the largest part of his essay detailing the difficulties that Christians have with such theological statements. These he refers to as the "anomalies of theological statements." They include the following.

First, the term *"God"* seems to function as a proper name but not one that can be used in direct reference. Crombie concludes that "the symbol 'God' might therefore be described as an *improper proper name*. . . . It is not easy to see how such a symbol could have a valid use" (40). He then goes on to point out that *"God"* seems to function like "a geometer's fiction," like the idea of a geometrical point. As he writes, "in a sense there could not be such a thing as a point [a thing both size-less and somewhere]," yet talk about points is useful in talking about spatial relationships.

Second, the language of theological statements is language not being used in its everyday sense. We talk about God loving and caring for his people. Yet, according to Crombie, "nothing which happens is allowed to necessitate the withdrawal of these statements, they are allowed to overrule all factual observations" (43). He continues: "How, in that case, can we ever learn what meaning to attach to the words in the predicate expression?" (43). These anomalies lead Crombie eventually to state that "God is a transcendent, infinite and incomprehensible being, in incomprehensible relationship with the familiar universe" (49).

Crombie argues, however, that this does not make theological language meaningless. He maintains that it may not be possible to fix the reference of theological discourse but that it is possible to fix "the reference-range." Crombie states: "Religion is connected . . . with ethics, cosmology, history and psychology. . . . It has nothing very direct to contribute to mathematics, literary criticism or marine biology" (52).

The question Crombie tries to answer is "What does theological language have to contribute to our understanding of those things?" Crombie's answer is that it brings to our consciousness the concept of spirit. Part of our experience of ourselves is the experience of a kind of physical/spiritual duality. We are definitely physical beings, but we also seem to be more than that. Talk about the functioning of our hearts and arteries and glands is useful and necessary, but so is talk about courage and love and responsibility. The latter way of talking requires a different vocabulary, one related to but not reducible to the talk about the former. It is such talk that the language of spirit and the language of God as Infinite Spirit supports. We are supported in our effort to be spiritual beings by communications from the Infinite Spirit. For the Christian, these communications include the history of Israel, the life and death of Christ, and the life of the Christian community (68). But might we not have our spirit life so informed without believing that these accounts are factually true? Wouldn't it be sufficient simply to look at the world as if they were true? Crombie states:

> People do not behave in real life quite as they behave in the books of Hardy, Dostoevsky, Kafka, Huxley; and yet it is possible for a man's understanding of real life to be deepened by reading their books. But what we learn from Kafka or Huxley is not that the real world is like the world they create; rather having traveled in imagination to a very different world, when we come back to the real world we see it a little differently, and the difference seems to be gain. . . . We might discover that our understanding of life was deepened by conceiving of it in Christian terms; in that case the Bible could be regarded as a work of "serious" fiction. . . . Of course that is not enough. . . . Creation, Redemption Judgement are not to be accepted as illuminating fables, but affirmed as faithful parables. (79)

This ends up being Crombie's formula for belief, "the affirming of the parables." Crombie states:

> That these parables deepen our understanding of the world is certainly one of our grounds for affirming them; it is by no means the whole content of that affirmation. To believe these doctrines [Creation, Redemption, Judgment] is not only to believe that they illuminate the facts that come within our view, but also to believe that they do so because they are revelatory of facts which lie outside our view. (79)

Crombie wants to affirm both sides of a difficult, if not paradoxical, situation:

> We must confess that we do not understand the relationship in which God stands to the world, but we must also claim the right to name it "creatorship" or "sustaining". The choice of the name is not arbitrary, although, since we do not understand the relation named, its use is in some way equivocal. . . . Our use of this image . . . is based on two things: . . . we find ourselves impelled to regard the events recorded in the Bible and found in the life of the Church as the communication of a transcendent being, and that the image is an essential part of this communication; secondly, . . . the more we try to understand the world in light of this image, the better our understanding of the world becomes. These two things conspiring together are our authority for the use of the image, and for our affirming it. (81)

I applaud several things in Crombie's essay: the honesty with which he lays out the anomalies and does not try to dodge their implications, and his pointing out that theological statements have a relevance over a fairly definite range of human experience and that this relevance is related to our way of understanding ourselves as fully moral, appreciative, responsive, and responsible beings.

I also have a small criticism. With reference to Crombie's example that one can't believe in Dr. Jones if one doesn't believe that there is a Dr. Jones, I agree. Crombie is right about that particularly if "believing in" means that I trust Dr. Jones's diagnoses or believe in his ability as a surgeon. But I can believe in the equality of all humans without believing that all humans are, in fact, equal. I can believe in the teachings of the Buddha without believing that Gautama Siddhartha actually said all the things he is credited with saying. I can be moved to change my life by Gully Jimson's perceptive comments without believing that Jimson is anything but a work of fiction. Crombie's argument here depends on the particular example he employs. A different example may, rather than supporting his argument, provide reason to question it. There are many cases where "belief in" does not require "belief that."

I would also raise several more substantial critical questions. First, is "affirming the parables" really the same thing as propositional belief? How do we "affirm" creatorship or sustaining if we do not understand the sense in which these terms may be applied to God? Perhaps we can, in some vague sense, affirm a statement. I can nod assent to a statement spoken in a language I do not speak, though we do not legally count such a thing as assent. But I fail to understand how one can claim to *believe* a proposition one cannot claim to understand. Crombie seems willing to admit the problems of understanding (the point of the anomalies) but not to give up the essential character of belief.

Second, is Crombie's argument finally an argument from biblical authority? Is the argument finally circular? In what sense are we "impelled" to use particular parables? Does the argument run something like this: we find ourselves impelled to believe these things because this is what we, in fact, believe? Is that really an argument form that Crombie would endorse? Would he endorse it for generalized use? I believe that Crombie's essay has come very close to the heart of the issue, but I believe that he backs away from the conclusions that his analysis necessitates. Crombie's essay is helpful in showing us where the problems lie but not very helpful in solving them.

A Theory of Religious Discourse

Thus far, we should have noted several things about religious language:

- It frequently relates a story but not just any kind of story. It is myth—that is, *it is a life-orienting story.*
- It is language about the present and the future as well as often about the past—that is, it is language simultaneously in the past, the present, and the future tenses.
- It is story connected essentially to ritual—that is, to enactment and performance. As Armstrong suggests as cited in the Introduction, it is like a musical score, a communication that is understood only when we hear it and see it played.

- It is visionary—that is, it shapes how we see the world.
- The story, the ritual enactment, the vision, all reorient us to the world—that is, they change how we act and how we treat the world and one another; they inform practice.

Any theory that would account for the meaning of religious discourse must take all of these things into account. The theory must be multidimensional, and it should show us how these dimensions are related to one another. These are, I believe, the five dimensions of religious language and religious meaning. It is (1) mythic; (2) it is poly-tensed (i.e., simultaneously in the past, present, and future tenses); (3) it is played out in ritual; (4) it is visionary, informing how we experience ourselves, one another and the world; and, consequently, (5) it is pragmatic (i.e., it is action and life shaping).

After hearing me talk about how story and ritual inform practice to complete the meaning of religious discourse, a student asked for an example. I talked about the Christian eucharistic meal. We have the story of Jesus sharing bread and wine with his disciples, and we have the ritual practice of partaking in the "Lord's Supper." The student then asked, "But when do we put that into practice?" I told him of experiences in three different Christian communities on three different continents—before the eucharistic meal, when the offering was being received, members of the congregation brought food to the altar. After the sharing of bread and wine among the members of the church, the trays of food were taken outside and shared with people in the streets. The story tells of receiving a precious gift and sharing, the ritual rehearses it, and then the congregation practices it. In these three dimensions, the purposes of God are revealed.

The student came back to the next class meeting and said, "I see how story, ritual, and practice work together in many cases. But I don't think it works that way always. With the most important informing Christian story, the resurrection of Jesus, we do have a ritual, namely the celebration of Easter. But *where do we practice resurrection?*" I asked the class to excuse me for two minutes while I ran upstairs to my office to fetch a book of poems. When I returned, I read to them Wendell Berry's "Manifesto: The Mad Farmer's Liberation Front" (1973).

Love the quick profit, the annual raise,
vacation with pay. Want more

of everything ready made. Be afraid
to know your neighbors and to die.
And you will have a window in your head.
Not even your future will be a mystery
any more. Your mind will be punched in a card
and shut away in a little drawer.
When they want you to buy something
they will call you. When they want you
to die for profit they will let you know.
So, friends, every day do something
that won't compute. Love the Lord.
Take all that you have and be poor.
Love someone who does not deserve it.
Denounce the government and embrace
the flag. Hope to live in that free
republic for which it stands.
Give your approval to all you cannot
understand. Praise ignorance, for what man
has not encountered he has not destroyed.
Ask the questions that have no answers.
Invest in the millennium. Plant sequoias.
Say that your main crop is the forest
that you did not plant,
that you will never live to harvest.
Say that the leaves are harvested
when they have rotted into mold.
Call that profit. Prophesy such returns.
Put your faith in the two inches of humus
that will build under the trees
every thousand years.
Listen to carrion—put your ear
close, and hear the faint chattering
of the songs that are to come.
Expect the end of the world. Laugh.
Laughter is immeasurable. Be joyful
though you have considered all the facts.

> So long as women do not go cheap
> for power, please women more than men.
> Ask yourself: Will this satisfy
> a woman satisfied to bear a child?
> Will this disturb the sleep of a woman near to giving birth?
> Go with your love to the fields.
> Lie easy in the shade. Rest your head
> in her lap. Swear allegiance
> to what is nighest your thoughts.
> As soon as the generals and the politicos
> can predict the motions of your mind,
> lose it. Leave it as a sign
> to mark the false trail, the way you didn't go. Be like the fox
> who makes more tracks than necessary,
> some in the wrong direction.
> Practice resurrection.

Of course, it was that last line I was heading toward. Someone, Berry at least, thinks resurrection can and ought to be practiced and, given the multiple images of the poem, thinks this happens whenever we choose for life rather than death, freedom rather than imperial control, the kingdom of God rather than the economy, love rather than manipulation, and whimsy, lunacy even, rather than what the culture counts as success.

FROM THE CLASSROOM: STUDENT QUESTIONS & RESPONSES

Q: I can imagine people who are outside of a religious community finding your account of religion as imagination-informed seeing as appealing. But I would also suppose that people inside of religious communities will find your substituting imagination for belief as shocking and appalling.

R: I'm sure you're right that many religious people will not like this approach. But the interesting thing is that I have been led to this view mainly by people inside of religious communities—like the people I quote in this text. These include people from Jewish, Christian, Buddhist, Taoist, and

Native American religious communities. Without the work of these people, I never would have found myself thinking this way. So it isn't just religious outsiders who are led in this direction.

On the other hand, if some "religious outsiders" find in this approach a reason to reexamine why they find themselves "outside," then the book will have been worth writing. I think of the book as being for anyone who is willing to question some assumptions and consider religious faith in a new light. Where they are religiously "located" is not a primary interest. Consider Kathleen Norris (discussed in chapter 1). Was she a religious insider or outsider? Or, was she an insider who thought she was an outsider?

Q: Is it possible for a religion to have two of the parts you mention but be lacking a third? Could it still be a religion? The example that I have in mind is a twelve-step recovery group. They certainly have a ritual: something like confession, something like a statement of reliance on some power beyond oneself, an embracing of one another in our fallible and wounded state, an intention to make amends and work on the problem, and so forth. The process can be life transforming as well. But, that I know of, there's no story told, no mythology.

R: That's a really good example. But it seems to me it is story informed as well. It just isn't a standard or written-down story, and it doesn't become part of a sacred text. But it's the story that each member tells. For example: "My name is Bob. I'm an alcoholic. My alcoholism lost me my job, ruined my marriage, and estranged me from my two kids. I've been sober for eight months and two weeks." In the process of the meeting, everyone tells a story. The stories are all different yet surprisingly alike. In the process of this telling, a kind of community is formed, a community where it is okay to be honest, to be who I really am. I think it's a great example of a religious community.

Q: If it's not all that important to literally believe the focal story, then why can't we just make up stories that can be ritualized and be life informing? Could there be a Dr. Seuss religion focused around *Yertle the Turtle*, *The Lorax*, and *Horton Hears a Who*?

R: That's a very creative suggestion. Right now, I can't see any reason why that couldn't occur. In fact, the religion might be preferable, practically speaking, to many religions that do exist or have existed.

QUESTIONS FOR CRITICAL REFLECTION

1. Kushner contrasts religion considered as "a something to be believed" with religion as "a way of seeing." Choose some significant religious story or one of the Psalms. What would it be like to read it as "a something to be believed"? As something to inform "a way of seeing"? Are these mutually exclusive? Can something be regarded in both ways simultaneously?

2. Are there some narratives in the Bible that just don't seem to work as "a way of seeing"? Are there some that don't seem to work as "a something to be believed"?

3. Why are we inclined to suppose that imagination is just about a realm of make-believe? Is it troublesome to discover that imagination informs the way we see reality in both the sciences and other rational pursuits? What interest does it serve to keep imagination trivial and to maintain that important things cannot be imagination informed?

4. The text gives several examples of imagination-informed ways of knowing—architecture, astronomy, Newton's physics, political and moral thought, map making. Can you think of other good examples of imagination-informed ways of knowing? Is the discipline you are studying in your major like that?

5. Hick characterizes faith as a kind of "experiencing-as." Isn't that also what is happening in many of the arts (e.g., seeing solid things as a play of lines or as patches of color)? Does that show that Hick is wrong, or does it actually support his argument?

6. Both Farrar and Crombie talk about theological language as a language of parable. What do you take that to mean? Are they affirming the same thing or something slightly different? What would it mean to read Jesus' birth narrative in Luke as if it were a parable? Is that what the poet is doing in the "Christmas Poem 2007"?

7. What are your thoughts about Wendell Berry's poem? Do all the things he recommends doing have anything to do with "practicing resurrection"? If not, then what would such a practice look like?

5. Rethinking the Rationality of Faith

The Question of the Rationality of Faith

If religious faith is primarily or essentially the belief that a divine being exists, then such faith is rational only if there are sufficient reasons to believe such a thing or if there are better reasons for believing than disbelieving such a thing. The key question, given this beginning assumption, becomes "Are there good reasons to believe in the existence of God?" The philosophy of religion has for centuries been a debate of the pros and cons of that argument on the assumption that this is the character of faith and the crucial question.

Throughout this book, we have tried to show that there is another way to look at it:

- We have tried to raise doubts about whether belief is the focal act of faith.
- We have questioned whether God-language is primarily referential.
- We have questioned whether existence is the appropriate term to be applied to God and whether the existence-of-God debate is interminable because it's ill conceived.
- We have questioned whether something other than propositional belief serves better as a description of what faith is and how it works in the life of the faithful.
- We have suggested that faith is better understood as a way of experiencing self and world that is imagination informed. We have tried to show that religious faith is very similar to much of science and moral and political thinking in this respect.

If any of these critical thoughts is well founded, we should reconsider what kind of discussion is relevant to examining the rationality of religious faith. That is the point of this final section: to revisit the question of the rationality of faith, informed by the discussions of recent chapters.

The best way to do this is to look back again at the examples of imagination-informed seeing we considered in chapter 4. Was it rational of Newton to premise his entire science on the paradigm of continuous straight-line motion? Was it rational of the drafters and signers of our nation's founding documents to premise their political arguments on the claim that all men are created equal? If, as we claim, these operations of mind are analogous to religious faith, then we might find in them a model for understanding how to ask about the rationality of faith.

Newton's Scientific Achievement Revisited

In the discussion of Newton in chapter 4 (see pp. 78–79), we said:

> Newton's first law of motion asserts that an object in motion will remain in motion in a straight line unless it is perturbed by some outside influence. But look around. Where is there an object that does this? The motion of stones and bowling balls is not eternal nor is it straight line. The movement of planets or the moon may seem eternal, but it's not straight-line motion either. Newton makes eternal straight-line motion the very premise of his system. Yet, an object that actually behaves as so described is a complete fiction. Why? Because the motion of every object is "perturbed." What is this perturbation that influences the motion of everything in the universe? Gravity.
>
> Newton's discovery was not to find some hidden thing. It was to look at the world in a different way, a way shaped by the hypothesis that normal motion was straight-line constant motion and that any other kind of motion needed to be explained. The moon does not move in a straight line; therefore, there must be some outside force sufficient to bend its path.
>
> Many of Newton's scientific contemporaries thought he had lost his mind. "Prove to us that straight-line constant motion is the norm. Show us where in nature such motion occurs?" they demanded. He could not. "Show us this force that you call gravity; it sounds like an occult explanation to us," they challenged. He could not show it except by pointing at everything. "Explain to us how the mass of the earth affects the motion of the moon at such a distance. Where's the cord? What's the mechanism of it?" they persisted. Newton had no answer.

What's interesting about this example is that, considered in one way, Newton's approach seems quite irrational. Newton premises motion under an ideal condition, where an object's motion is not perturbed by anything else. The problem is that this ideal circumstance does not anywhere exist; Newton cannot show a single instance of unperturbed straight-line motion. And that is precisely Newton's point. Even the motion of remote and apparently isolated bodies, such as the moon and the planets, is perturbed, namely, by the force he called gravity. This force cannot be seen, and it cannot be described; we can only say how it influences the motions of other things that "attract proportional to their masses and inversely to the square of the distance between them."

If we go looking for gravity, we can't find it. It is not a thing to be found. If we go looking for the paradigm case of motion, an object moving continuously in a straight line, we can't find that either. All we find are "perturbed" objects, objects under the influence of this invisible and "occult" force called gravity. How could this possibly be rational? How could it possibly be good science? This is what several of Newton's contemporaries were asking.

What makes it not only good but great science is what can be seen and understood by means of it. Employing this little paradigm, Newton was able to come up with mathematical formulae that would explain and predict the motions of the moon, the planets, and terrestrial projectiles as well.

The rationality of the system is not its correspondence with an observed reality so much as it is its power to inform intelligently the way we see and know the physical world. It is its explanatory power that makes it a model for science. When, through careful observation, scientists discovered some things that Newton's theory did not explain, then they looked for alternative explanations. Newton's discovery was not finding a new and hitherto unknown reality but finding a new way to look at all of reality. This new way was rational in proportion to its fruitfulness.

Newton's account, evaluated as a description, is irrational. Newton's account, regarded as a vision-shaping paradigm, is a work of genius.

The Democratic Achievement Revisited

I don't think we know for sure who was the original source of the line "that all men are created equal." It may have been written by Jefferson, or it may have been spoken by Franklin or Adams or one of the other founders. Whoever the source, its inclusion in the Declaration of Independence was endorsed by all those present. The document says: "We hold these truths to be self-evident, that all men are created equal, that they are endowed by their Creator with certain unalienable rights, that among these are life, liberty and the pursuit of happiness." As we said in chapter 1, it would be a mistake to take this statement as a true empirical report because, in fact, people are unequal in so many different ways. The truth of the statement is not the truth of a conclusion based on observation but a premise that shapes observation. It shapes how we regard humans and their actual differences, and it says to us that, regarding humans' basic rights, there are no differences that count. Could an outlook based on such an obviously untrue statement possibly be rational? Empirically speaking, it would be more accurate to start with a statement about humans' inequalities and to state, as Thomas Hobbes did, that because of these differences we are all in a continual state of virtual war with one another.

Once again, regarded as a description, the egalitarian premise is quite irrational. But regarded as a vision-shaping paradigm, it is a work of genius. The rationality of the Declaration's premise is demonstrated by the institutions that it gave rise to—the rule of law rather than the rule of rank, representative government rather than divinely ordained government, a bill of rights that applies to individuals rather than a statement of rights that are the sole possession of the state and an elite. How do we look at persons and governments and courts as a consequence of this premise? It's that new way of seeing that either justifies or proves mistaken the paradigm on which it depends.

Both of these paradigms—Newton's ideal of continuous straight-line motion and Jefferson's ideal of humans endowed by their creator with equality and rights—inform a productive and usable vision of respective realities. Neither describe observable realities; both apply in spite of the fact that actual objects and persons do not correspond to the ideal they describe. Both reshape how we view the world, and both are paradigms of scientific and political reasoning. It would have been a great waste of time for Newton to attempt to demonstrate the descriptive truth of his premise. Newton is not claiming that "somewhere in the universe there is an object that does this." He is saying that "all objects are to be seen in light of this premise." It would have been a waste of time for Jefferson to have tried to verify his premise as though it were an empirical claim. Jefferson was not saying that "somewhere in the world there are two people who are absolutely equal." He was saying, "Look at everybody from this point of view, and you won't anymore count their inequalities as politically or legally relevant."

What makes these approaches in their respective fields rational? What makes them exemplars of scientific and political thinking? It is their power to reshape the way the world is seen and the productivity of the resulting visions.

If we go looking for gravity, we won't find it. If we go looking for the paradigm-making object, we won't find that either. What we may find is a world re-visioned in terms of that paradigm. If we go looking for equal persons, we won't find them, but what we may find is a world re-visioned in terms of the equality paradigm

If we go looking for God, we will not find her or him. What we may find is a world and a self transformed in terms of the God paradigm. We may then see the cosmos in awe and wonder, and see the world and our days in it as a gift received with thanksgiving. We may see other humans as our brothers and sisters, we may see the ordinary as deep with meaning, we may behold ourselves as essentially connected, we may see every life as redeemable, we may find strength and hope in the midst of pain and fear, and we may find every gift increased by sharing.

We cannot evaluate the rationality of religious faith by examining the correspondence of religious beliefs to reality. For one thing, the "reality" they supposedly refer to is not accessible to us. But we have now seen that it may be a serious mistake to have regarded religious language as descriptive of such a "reality" at all. Religious language, we have argued, is better regarded as shaping a way of seeing everything rather than describing a special something to go looking for. God-language, like Newton's gravity language and Jefferson's equality language, does not describer some verifiable "matter of fact," as Pojman (2001) put it, so much as it shapes conception, perception, and experience of everything there is.

Thus, the evaluation of religious faith is not verification so much as it is vindication. We go beyond fruitlessly asking, "Does this correspond to the facts," and need to begin to ask, "How does this work to shape experience and life itself?" Does the experience-shaping God paradigm work? Does it shape and transform life effectively? Does it enable us to live well and fully?

The Pragmatic Examination of Religion: James, Nietzsche, Marx, and Freud

Though only William James is thought of as a pragmatist, in the strict sense of the word, each of these four thinkers brings a pragmatic test to their examination of religion. Because their conclusions are different, we can see what a creative variety a pragmatist understanding of religion may imply.

William James (1842–1910)

William James did not invent the philosophical movement called pragmatism, but he quickly became its principal spokesperson. "Pragmatism," James wrote, "[is] first of all a method; and second a . . . theory of what is meant by truth" (2000, 33). The method is to test every idea by asking, "What practical difference would it make if this were true?" The pragmatic theory of truth is to understand the term, not as the static *relation* between idea and reality but as the *processes* of validation, verification, and justification.

For James, truth is more an active verb than it is a noun or an adjective. The test of an idea is to ask, "What can one do with it?" The test of the truth of an idea is the various testing processes. In simple cases, we test a sentence such as "The cat is sleeping on the mat" by looking for the cat. But in other cases, we are not in a position to simply look and see. If our question is "Which theory most adequately explains the common spiral shape of galaxies?" we may have to enter into a long and complex process of justification. We evaluate theories by what they explain, what they leave unexplained, what they imply, and what fruit they bear in helping us discover new things about the cosmos. If we're asking, "Does Freud's theory of the tri-partite structure of the psyche makes sense?" we have no observable "reality" against which to check its correspondence. But we can ask, "Is the theory fruitful?" and "Is it suggestive of future research and insight?" and "Is it therapeutic?" James would say that all of these questions are verification/justification procedures. And all of them, he would add, are species of the more general question "Does this idea or theory work?"

Many times in his writings, James addresses this question to religion. In his study of a religious tradition, he raises the questions "What does this myth or dogma or world-view look like as a guide to life?" and "What does it amount to when it is put into practice?"

James looks at religious beliefs and philosophical world-views as dividing themselves into opposing alternatives along lines established by basic questions: Is reality fundamentally unitary or pluralistic, one or many? Is the world basically a place one can find oneself at home, or is it a place full of risk and adventure? Is the world fundamentally a place of necessity or of possibility, adjustment, or change? Is it basically good or bad? Which makes more sense, optimism or pessimism? James sees the world religions as basically addressing these questions and producing a life pattern in which these alternatives are then lived out. James appreciates why different people, with different psychological makeups, would choose one or the other.

But James is not afraid to indicate his own preferences. He seems to prefer pluralism over monism, risk and adventure over safety and security, possibility over necessity. He rejects both pessimism and optimism as tending toward the necessity end of the spectrum and argues instead for a middle position that he calls *meliorism* (2000, 125). The world is not determined to become either the best or the worst. What happens will occur because of our efforts to change things for the better. Meliorism is a council to effective action. Neither optimism nor pessimism makes sense of effort because they both assume that "what will happen will happen." They are, he believes, councils of quietism and despair.

Is religion, from James's point of view, a good thing or a bad thing? James's response is to say that the answer cannot be given wholesale, because it depends on the needs of the person in the world. James suggests that it's like trying to answer the question "Are morphine and other pain killers good things or bad?" Sometimes they are exactly what one needs to manage one's situation. Other times they are dangerous and harmful things indeed. James also thinks that no dogmatic answer about the value of religion is available. He writes: "We do not yet know which type of religion will work out best in the long run. The various over-beliefs of men, their several faith-ventures, are in fact what are needed in order to bring the evidence in" (2000, 131).

Friedrich Nietzsche (1844–1900)

The work of Nietzsche is nearly impossible to summarize. Much of his writing is aphoristic rather than developmental or argumentative. It takes the form of short, somewhat disconnected paragraphs intended to provoke thought and interpretation. Nietzsche seemed to devalue consistency. Consequently, not only do his different works say different things, but he will sometimes end by critiquing an assumption he was making at the beginning.

Nietzsche did not critique theistic arguments. He did not critique religion on the grounds that it was a myth or fiction. Nietzsche was himself an accomplished myth maker and a storyteller. The question that interested him was how the story shapes the lives and psyches of those who tell it and hear it.

Nietzsche's critique of Judaism and Christianity is not that the two religions are not true but that they are humanly debilitating. Their ethic and their beliefs give support to what Nietzsche sees as human failings—humility, slavishness, timidity, fearfulness, otherworldliness, weakness, poverty, being "poor in spirit," and so forth. At the same time, the religions regard the opposites of these "virtues"—strength, vitality, aggressiveness, struggle, worldliness, spirit—as sins. Judaism and Christianity (and many other religions?) are expressions of what he calls a "slave morality," a morality written by the oppressed class, motivated by resentment by the weak of the naturally strong and healthy (the noble morality). Nietzsche thinks that these religions do a splendid job of comforting and encouraging the weak, the victims of life—and that that is what is wrong with them. The problem is not that the religions fail to promote a mode of life but that they succeed so well—to advance a mode of life that Nietzsche sees as weak, pitiful and, in some senses, subhuman.

Nietzsche, in *Beyond Good and Evil* (1999), writes:

> Religions side with the defectives.... They confirm the rights of all those who suffer from life as though it were a disease; they would like to render invalid and impossible any other sentiments besides theirs.... They have preserved too much of what should have perished.... To turn upside down all valuations—that is what they had to do! To shatter the strong, to infect great hopes, to cast suspicion on the enjoyment of beauty, to break down everything autonomous, manly, victorious, dominating ... and bend it over into uncertainty, distress of conscience, and self-destruction—to reverse every bit of love for the earth and things earthly ... into hatred of things earthly and of the earth: this was the self-assumed task of the church. (70–71)

Nietzsche views positively any mythology that celebrates strength, vitality, exuberance, and creativity and that embraces the earthly and celebrates the whole of life, including both its joys and its tragedies. He sees two myths as doing that—one he calls eternal recurrence, the view that the present moment equals eternity, and the other he calls, in German, *der Ubermensch*, the over-human, the ideal embodiment of the courageous human strengths he envisioned.

Karl Marx (1818–1883)

Karl Marx begins his philosophical argument in a very different place from Nietzsche, with a different set of assumptions and vocabulary. But Marx is led to a conclusion not all that different from Nietzsche's: the problem of religion is not that it does not work but that it works too well.

Religion, from Marx's view, performs two different functions for two different classes of people. First, for those who are doing well—those who own the means of production and control the economy for their own advantage—religion serves as an ideological justification of their status and power. For example, not only am I in a position to profit from your labor, but God endorses my success and your poverty. Second, for those who are oppressed and suffering, the promise of heaven and a life to come serve as a painkiller. They make an otherwise horrible situation bearable. Marx wrote:

> Religious suffering is at the same time an expression of real suffering and a *protest* against real suffering. Religion is the sigh of the oppressed creature, the sentiment of a heartless world, and the soul of soulless conditions. It is the opium of the people.
>
> The abolition of religion as the illusory happiness of men is a demand for their real happiness. *The call to abandon their illusions about their happiness is a call to abandon the condition that requires illusions.* The criticism of religion is, therefore, the embryonic criticism of this vale of tears of which religion is the halo. . . . The criticism of religion disillusions man so that he will hitherto work without illusions. (1977, 43–44, 52–53)

But isn't religion also a source of concern, care, and positive change for the oppressed of the earth? Marx isn't convinced. About Christianity, he writes:

> The social principles of Christianity . . . have had eighteen hundred years to develop. . . . The social principles of Christianity have justified slavery, glorified the serfdom of the middle ages and know, when

necessary, how to defend the oppression of the proletariat although they make a pitiful face over it . . . [and] preach the necessity of the ruling and an oppressed class, and all they have for the latter is the pious wish that the former will be charitable. (1964, 83–84)

Sigmund Freud (1856–1939)

Religion is a theme in many of the works of Sigmund Freud, best known for his development of psychoanalysis and the theory on which it is based. Freud saw humans as being driven by basic animal instincts, including sex and the desire to do violence to one's sexual competitors. Yet, humans live in societies that are structured in such a way as to control both of these drives. We create external laws and objectify them to control ourselves. We are thus victims of a double problem. Frustrated by our inability to express our natural drives, we are also victimized by the authority structures themselves. The result is neurotic sublimation of the drives, and psychotic attachment to and rebellion against the objectified authority. Religion, of course, plays a role in and is an example of both.

Freud, in *The Future of an Illusion* (1964), wrote:

> The gods retain their threefold task: they must exorcise the terrors of nature, they must reconcile men to the cruelty of Fate, particularly as it is shown in death, and they must compensate them for the sufferings and privations which civilized life in common has imposed on them. (24)

In the monotheistic religions, Freud argues, God is the objectification of the father figure. Like the relationship of the child to the father, the relationship to God is not simple:

> The child's relationship to its father is colored by a peculiar ambivalence. The father himself constitutes a danger for the child, perhaps because of its earlier relation to its mother. Thus it fears him no less than it longs for him and admires him. The indications of this ambivalence . . . are deeply imprinted in every religion. . . . When the growing individual finds that he is destined to remain a child forever, that he can never do without protection against strange superior powers, he lends those powers the features belonging to the figure of the father; he creates for himself the gods whom he dreads . . . and whom he nevertheless entrusts with his own protection. (34–35)

In addition, religion is an illusion. Freud wrote: "We call a belief an illusion when a wish fulfillment is a prominent factor in its motivation, and in doing so we disregard its relation to reality, just as the illusion sets no store by verification" (49). Religion, Freud concludes, is a form of infantilism and a kind of learned helplessness. Rather than appealing to an illusional way to deal with problems, Freud argues that we should recognize our problems for what they are and deal with them realistically and straightforwardly. A young woman (who may have grown up hearing the stories of Snow White and Cinderella) might shape her life around the hope that someday a prince will come and rescue her from her miseries and frustrations. Such an illusion may comfort her and may make her life bearable. But therein lies the problem. Like those of Nietzsche and Marx, Freud's critique of religion is not that the mythology does not work but that it works too well. Like the girl whose "someday my prince will come" illusion keeps her from dealing realistically with her problems, religion works to do the same. Religion is not an *enabling* story, Freud argues, but a *disabling* one, keeping the faithful in an infantile relation to the realities of self and world.

All four of the thinkers discussed here—James, Nietzsche, Marx, and Freud—bring a pragmatist critique to religion. All of them agree that the heart of any religious tradition is the kind of life it inspires and the difference it makes in practice. They differ in their critiques depending on the kind of life they would like to see humans live.

Nietzsche is surely right in pointing out that religion can be used as a support for those who would make a virtue of their own weakness. He's also right in pointing out that it's often motivated by resentment and that believers are often sustained by the thought that someday the tables will be turned when "those people" are punished for the sins they enjoy today. Marx is surely right in pointing out that religion has been used as a justification for gross inequality and injustice. The Hindu belief in karma and the protestant Christian endorsement of wealth and privilege as signs of divine election are two of the most obvious examples. Freud is surely right in pointing out that religion can be a handicapping illusion supporting the juvenile believer in his or her passive and dependent state.

The question we must ask about all of these critiques is whether these *possible uses* of religion capture their essence or whether they are, in fact, *abuses* of the religious ideal. It's hardly fair to critique a medicine on the grounds that one might overdose on it. Nor is it fair to critique automobiles on the grounds that they might be used for vehicular homicide. Are all religions essentially what these three critics say they are? Or, are there ways that each of the religions considered may be lived out that avoid the problems that Nietzsche, Marx, and Freud so vividly identify?

Do Judaism, Christianity, Hinduism, and Buddhism turn a blind eye to the causes of inequality and economic injustice, as Marx claims? Are they, by their very nature, life denying and earth despising and resentment driven, as Nietzsche claims? Do religions result in and reinforce passivity and learned infantile helplessness, as Freud argues? We can certainly produce examples of religious persons who fit the descriptions Nietzsche, Marx, and Freud identify. But we can also, I would argue, produce exemplars of religious persons who are strong, courageous, bold, and healthy in a way Nietzsche would have admired. We can find exemplars of religious persons who are active change agents for equality and economic justice whom Marx would have been pleased to meet. We can find religious persons who are living active, responsible, and psychologically healthy lives in a way that Freud would have admired.

Merold Westphal, in his excellent book *Suspicion and Faith* (1993), responds to Freud, Nietzsche, and Marx by accusing them of plagiarism on the grounds that all of their sharpest criticisms of religion appear in the Bible itself. He writes:

> The Christian Bible is surely the most anti-religious of all the world's scriptures. . . . In the old Testament the prophets tell the people that God cannot stand their worship. In the New Testament, Paul wages war against the religion of being good, to which James responds with a sharp critique of those who would abuse the gospel of grace. But the most thoroughly anti-religious texts in the Bible are the Gospel narratives in which the piety of the Pharisees, of the Jerusalem power elite which was dominated by Sadducees, and of Jesus' own disciples is relentlessly exposed as self-righteous and self-centered. . . . It is for this reason that I accuse the modern atheists of plagiarism, since they tend to repeat in their battle with biblical religion the criticisms already directed to pious Jews and Christians by the Bible. (265)

The real meaning of a religion is the kind of life that is informed by it. The fact that a given religion can lead to very different embodiments shows that we should not take the name of a single religion, whether "Christian," "Hindu," "Muslim," or something else, as the primary indicator. Both Gandhi and those complicit in his assassination called themselves Hindu, yet there was a world of difference between them. Both Dietrich Bonhoeffer and the official church of the Third Reich were Lutheran Christians in name, yet there was a world of difference between them as well. This may lead us to conclude that these generic names do more harm than good, hiding huge differences behind a common nomination.

We understand a story fully by seeing the life form it informs. We understand the life form also by hearing the story. They mutually inform each other. Myth is well defined, therefore, as life-informing story, and religion is well defined as a story-informed life. Both of them, story and life, need to be present before any judgment of a religion can be made.

Some Problems with the Pragmatic Critique

About four years ago, a vice president at the university where I teach began his presentation to the fall faculty workshop with the words "I'd like to introduce you to the incoming class—the graduating class of 2010." He then proceeded to project several charts of statistics. We learned about their SAT and ACT scores, their rank in their high school class, their average family income, the probability that they would graduate in four years, the probability of their having or getting an STD, the probability of their already owing over $5,000 on their charge card, the probability of their not knowing the name of a single person on the Supreme Court, and so forth. Nearly every statistic imaginable was provided.

Had we met the class of 2010? Many of us would have been quick to point out that persons are not statistics and that it would be a mistake, on our part, to think of them as such. What we had before us was two different ways of seeing students: as bundles of statistics or as something that resists reduction to statistics, namely, as persons.

Both of these ways of seeing are imagination informed. Both require an experiencing-as of the sort Hick (1969) talks about (see our discussion in chapter 4). Both of them, I would submit, have a certain usefulness. Both of them are considered by some, at least, as *the* picture of reality. Both of them provide temptations to participate in a kind of reductionism, although in the modern world the temptation to think of reality as equivalent to the measurable and countable is by far the more dominant and, I believe, the more dangerous.

Many ways of seeing-as are justified as tools. I would count statistics, economics, logic, and mechanics as such extremely useful tools. But, I would argue, each becomes a fallacy if regarded as more than a tool; if, that is, it is regarded as the whole of reality or regarded as an adequate life-shaping philosophy.

Are these views rational? As ways of seeing—that is, as tools—both are rational because they are fruitful, useful, and significant. As *the* way of seeing, as *the* picture of reality, neither is. As useful, imagination-shaped ways of experiencing, both are justified. I personally would say that, given the modern temptation to reduce the real to the quantifiable, the personalist view will get my support and my loyalty and my commitment. I am a user of statistics; a skeptical user, I should add. But I am committed to a world shaped by person-language and person concepts. Should we lose this way of speaking and thinking and acting, we would have lost something essential to being human. Should we lose statistics, we would certainly be less clever. Perhaps there are even insights about the human condition we would miss, but I doubt we would be less human.

My conclusion is that statistics is a useful way of looking at the world. It is a useful tool. But it becomes downright dangerous when it is taken to be the whole of reality. The same thing is true of economics. Economics makes a very good servant, but when it becomes the master and not the servant, then human life and our communities and planet may be put at risk.

Should we say something similar about religion? Can it be life enhancing? Yes, I think it can. Can it be life destroying? Yes, that too is possible. Should it be regarded as a useful tool? As a servant but not a master? Surely, many seriously religious people would object to such a placement.

Preliminary Conclusions

Even though we have not yet reached the end of our analysis, let's see what point we have reached in our examination. Based on the above analysis, we may say the following:

1. Faith statements are to be treated not so much as conclusions—that is, the outcome of evidentiary arguments—as they are life- and thought-transforming ways of imagining.

2. Faith statements are thought shaping and experience shaping. If used well, they give us a new way of understanding ourselves, the world, and the others we encounter in the world. Faith is not so much the belief in some new thing as it is a transformed way of seeing all things. Or, in the case where we do encounter a new thing, its significance lies in the power it has to transform our way of seeing all things.
3. It is a great waste of time and energy to try to justify faith claims by any method of verification or to prove them by any argument. Faith is vindicated, not verified. We are not *persuaded* of the truth of a religious outlook so much as we are *converted* to it and converted by it. That conversion occurs when our way of seeing and thinking is reshaped. Coming to faith is the adoption of a new paradigm, or perhaps its better to say it's like *being adopted by* a new paradigm.
4. We judge the rationality of these religious ways of seeing by their power to shape and reshape our lives. They are judged pragmatically by their productivity and fruitfulness, by their world-shaping and life-shaping power. They are vindicated by their use in life shaping and world shaping.
5. Faith is justified by the way it shapes and changes life. Life is changed in conjunction with changes in oneself and the world one experiences. There are many examples of such ways of talking in the Hebrew Scriptures and in the letters of Paul and other early Christian writers:

Behold I create a new heaven and a new earth. (Isaiah 56)

In Christ we are new creatures. (2 Corinthians 5)

And I saw a new heaven and a new earth. (Revelation 21)

Fruitfulness as a Criterion?

Just a little bit of reflection will show us that fruitfulness is not a univocal standard or criterion. The question always remains to be asked, "Fruitful in doing what? Productive in what way? What fruits are to be counted?"

I'm sure there were (and are) critics of the Declaration of Independence. They may be able to see the egalitarian premise at work there. But unlike those who laud democracy and its fruits, they might say, "This is how the exclusive rights of royalty and gentry were lost," or "This is where the roots of anti-slavery and women's equality movements were planted." Rather than seeing these as positive outcomes, some may see them as negative outcomes flowing from the egalitarian premise.

One might regard the Genesis creation narrative as a paradigm in a similar way. One may draw the conclusion that this world-shaping story gives us a world in which all humans have the same ultimate parentage. We are all ultimately brothers and sisters; consequently, other ways we have of dividing ourselves—racially, ethnically, nationally, and so forth—are less a part of our fundamental human identity than is our being of one family. Someone who sees the implications of such a premise may either have a cause to rejoice in it or see this as reason to reject it. How we treat others in spite of their differences always is a fruit of our religiously inspired way of seeing. One set of religious premises may mold us into fierce chauvinists living in an us/them world; another may mold us into people who always strive to move beyond difference and who are always critical of us/them patterns of thought and action.

In the days following the 9/11 attacks, as we were learning that the destruction was the work of Islamic extremists, my son said, "I think the world would be better off without religious believers." I pointed out that not all religious faithful act that way and not all are fueled by hatred and us/them ways of looking at the world. "Just the same," he said, "the question remains whether religious faithful don't do more harm than good." I couldn't, and still can't, completely answer my son's question. In some ways, it's too general to be answered. Were he to put it in a more specific form, we might begin to answer it—for example, "The kind of Shinto that made possible emperor worship and Japanese nationalism—did that faith do more harm than good?" But I do believe that he was asking a good question. This is the way the question about the rationality of religious faith ought to be asked. It ought to be a question about the life of the faithful, not about evidences for or against the existence of God or gods named in worship.

I know many religious faithful think that such a question ought not to be asked at all. If the whole point of human life is to be obedient to God (i.e., to the view of God presented in one's religious tradition), then to even question whether such faith is a good idea is a kind of gross unfaithfulness, perhaps even blasphemy. Asking the question suggests that there is some way of answering the question apart from the religious tradition and the understanding of the will of God it presents.

Imagine a person who believes it is his religious duty to destroy the infidels of the world, or a person who believes that it is his religious duty to destroy the world itself. I would say that such a view is disastrous, destructive, and horrible. I would hope that people would seriously question the premises of such a belief and be led to abandon it. The fact that it would fuel a world of religious chauvinism, hatred, warfare, and mass annihilation is reason enough to declare it a kind of madness. But some religious faithful cannot get themselves to the place of even asking such a question. For them, the critical examination of religious faith is itself a religious impossibility. For such persons, the question is a gross impiety. The question for them is not whether faith is rational but whether rationality is faithful. But, of course, it isn't just religious ideologues who are incapable of critical questioning. Unfortunately, we meet political ideologues whose zeal for their own views seems to have wiped out rationality altogether.

A few decades ago, I had a student who, after an overdose on some combination of drugs, "flipped out." He was convinced that all the people he knew well and cared about had been replaced by imposters. So, though he was calm enough around total strangers, he became extremely paranoid and, ultimately, violent around those of us who were close to him. Eventually, he was confined in a psychiatric ward and put into restraints. Over a period of two months, he "came down" from his bad trip. Through this process, I visited him frequently. He began by refusing to believe that I was who I claimed to be. At one point, he declared me to be the arch-demon of the conspiracy to harm him. It was difficult to watch him in such a state. I finally came to realize that his behavior was completely rational based on his paranoid assumption. If his family and friends had been replaced by imposters, then his fear of us and his violent reaction to us made perfect sense. He lived in an internally consistent world. Within that world, he was perfectly sane and his actions and reactions were rational. The problem was that this world itself was false. Yet, there was no proving this to him. The more we tried to show care and concern for him, the more paranoid he became, taking our show of concern as an attempt to deceive him.

In the weeks of his recovery, I had many long discussions with him in which we explored the epistemology of his delusion. Was there anything I could do to prove to him that I was Dr. Christenson, his philosophy teacher? Every test we devised I passed, yet he read this as our being extremely devious and clever. His enemies had obviously kidnapped the real Tom Christenson and emptied his memory and mind into this imposter. This just confirmed his paranoia. It did nothing to remove it. Later, he was able to carry on this dialogue himself and began doubting his view of the world.

One can't give reasons for being rational. Every reason given already supposes a commitment to rationality. One can't give ethical reasons for being ethical. Every reason supposes a commitment to some ethical principles. If one gives prudential reasons for being ethical, on the other hand, then it isn't at all clear that one has made the hearer more ethical, just more prudential. The process of argument needs to show that the hearer already has ethical concerns and already sees things (to some degree) from an ethical point of view. Giving religious reasons for being religious is likewise circular. "You should be religious because God wants you to" will persuade no one who isn't already worried about the will of God. So all of these things—ethics, religious faith, and even rationality itself—require a kind of "leap of faith" in order to get going. One finds oneself already immersed in them. Or, one becomes converted to them rather than argued into them. And that conversion takes place by seeing how the life of the religious, ethical, and rational person is shaped and lived. I do not know anything else that can be appealed to in the final analysis.

To admit that religious faith may be completely a-rational, world destructive, and supra-ethical is surely to have dislocated religious faith from its connection with human life and well-being. It's to lose one's ability to be religiously concerned with human well-being and to lose one's ability to humanely critique religious faith. Faith might, at that point, have become logically unassailable, but it has at the same time become humanly uninteresting and indistinguishable from a kind of madness. To remove faith from the domain of rationality and morality is logically possible, but it is humanely impossible. As much as I admire the thought of Søren Kierkegaard, it is here that we part company. A risky faith requiring life commitment I can admire and understand; an insane and inhumane one I cannot.

We've all heard accounts of religious groups that end up "proving their faithfulness" by participating in some kind of suicide cult. For such persons, unquestioning faithfulness has become the only virtue and the words of the founder or leader the only measure of truth. Within that framework, the actions of the members may appear rational. From any other point of view, however, they seem like insanity. Such faith is, epistemologically at least, very similar to the "bad trip" of my former student.

Religious faith is rational (*if* it is) not because there is good evidence for its putative claims but because those ideas imaginatively shape a responsible and viable view of being human in the world. The point of religious faith is the fulfillment of human life.

Faith and the Fulfillment of the Human

"The point of religious faith is the fulfillment of human life." This statement ended the previous section. It is, I believe, both profound and potentially frightening, depending on how it is understood.

When I was about ten or eleven years old, I was part of a Sunday school class taught by a member of the congregation we attended. The teacher (I'll refer to him as Mr. S) was a local business man in his early fifties. He told us that if we gave our lives to Jesus, as he had done, we too could become successful businessmen, as he had. He had gone, in a ten-year period, from being a vacuum cleaner salesman to being the owner of four businesses and one of the major real estate investors in the area. His conversion and his faith in Jesus, he said, had been the key to his newfound success.

As I said at the outset, I was only a kid at the time, probably a fifth-grader. But even then, I knew there was something the matter with Mr. S's story. I knew that discipleship often required that people make serious sacrifices. I knew the stories of martyrs and others who bore a heavy burden of responsibility and suffering because of their faith. Becoming Christian certainly was not just a means to financial success and personal or social well-being as the culture defined it. I also understood, though I might not have been able to express it then, that the point of faith was to lead us beyond our own selfishness, not to the fulfillment of our own selfishness. If I had decided to become a Christian for the reasons Mr. S gave us, I might indeed have become rich, but I most certainly wouldn't have become a Christian. I would have become a person who used Christianity to fulfill his own greedy goals. Christianity would have been a means at most, not an end. I remember a student in an ethics class who said, "Give me some really good selfish reasons why I should care about anyone else." I had the good sense not to give him any. Had I succeeded in providing him with the reasons he demanded, I would not have made him other-concerned; I would have just confirmed his egoism.

So, when I read the sentence that opens this section, it gives me the shivers. I know that it can be read to say what Mr. S was saying to us: that Christian faith is a good bet because it leads to success in business, a beautiful new car, a large swimming pool, and so froth. It leads, in other words, to what Mr. S saw as the fulfillment of human life.

At one point in my life, I began playing tennis to advance my health. My doctor said, "You need more exercise. Why don't you try tennis? It gives you the aerobic workout you need plus lots of stretching and lower back work that will benefit you." So I did. After a few weeks, I also saw my game improving, so instead of spending most of my time chasing missed shots, I actually started being competitive, at least with the folks I found to play with. After about a year of play, I entered a senior doubles tournament with a friend and we did pretty well. The following summer, I played fairly often and looked for more challenging opponents. One weekend, I played two fierce matches with a new friend. By the end of the second day, I had blisters on my feet, had skinned my elbows and knees, and had finally sprained my foot. When I hobbled into my doctor's office the following week, he asked where the truck was that had hit me. I explained that all this occurred playing tennis. He laughed and said, "The idea was that you would play tennis to advance your health and take care of your body, not put your body at risk."

Indeed, that had been the point. What had happened? What started out being a means (playing tennis) to an end (bodily well-being) had itself turned into an end. Tennis was something that I had come to love so much that I was willing to sacrifice my skin and joints to the end of playing tennis well. A conversion had taken place—a conversion that most, if not all, athletes have undergone. Who hasn't heard a team member, bloodied and staggering in the fourth quarter, plead, "Send me in, Coach"?

When my oldest son was in his young teen years, we'd host a neighborhood weekend football game in our large backyard. Many weekends in a row, the game would end with a Sunday afternoon trip to the emergency room. The question got to be not whether the trip would be made but who would need the stitches or cast or concussion check this week? My wife told us that we were crazy to take part in an activity that put our bodies so at risk. It didn't seem to do any good to explain to her that there was little point in playing if we weren't going to "put ourselves into the game." "You're certainly doing that," she said, "but can't you see that you're crazy?"

In case the game-playing examples do not connect, many other examples can be found. There are some kids who have to be bribed to practice their musical instruments. "No TV until you've practiced for half an hour," the parent insists. But there are kids who would much rather play their instruments than watch TV. For them, practice is not a means to TV. Music is what they love, and TV counts for little, if anything. A child who starts out needing an extrinsic motivator to do music can be converted into a child for whom music is the motivator. At the outset, the child is bribed by TV time into practicing the instrument. Later, the youth turns off the TV in order to make music. A conversion has occurred.

Let us return to the example of Mr. S. Is it possible that, even though he "became a Christian" in order to get rich, he had somewhere along the way been converted to a life in Christ where his riches mattered little and he was willing to put them all to work in the service of sharing the love of God? Is it possible that his story turns, like the life of St. Francis, at the point where all his goods and possessions are put aside for a life given fully to his faith? It is possible. If it occurred, do not ask me to explain how it happened. The most I can say is something about conversion, or simply reiterate the nonexplanatory comment "miracle occurs here."

Let us look at an extreme example of such a conversion: the person who is willing to sacrifice his or her own life in the service of his or her faith. Such persons include martyrs of the early church, as well as Martin Luther King Jr. as a more contemporary example. But almost every day, the news is also filled with stories of young Muslims who blow themselves up delivering death to the infidel and the enemies of God. Putting one's life on the line in the service of God—from the point of view of faith, is anything more praiseworthy? Or, should my wife's words again be spoken: "Can't you see that you're crazy?"

We might attempt to avoid the case of violent religious extremists by saying that the opening statement must always be understood in its full moral sense: the fulfillment of the human includes the whole human community, not just the fulfillment of a single person or a single sect or party within that community. I am tempted to go in that direction and say that the violent destruction of the evil party (no matter who they are) can never ultimately serve the fulfillment of the human in its full moral sense. But at the same time, I realize that all kinds of violent acts have been and are justified on exactly such grounds. From the Crusades to more recent campaigns against "the axis of evil" and "the devil's army," the explanation has been given that it is not just *our* welfare that is being pursued but the welfare of the whole civilized world, or at least that part of it that God loves.

Faith, at least many of the forms of it with which I am acquainted, transforms the person who encounters it. I think again of the hymn in the *Lutheran Book of Worship* that reads, "Shepherd me, O God, beyond my wants, beyond my fears, from death into life." Imagine someone discovering himself or herself singing that verse. We can easily imagine ourselves praying to be delivered from our fears and to have our wants fulfilled. But can we imagine ourselves saying, shepherd me *beyond* my fears and *beyond* my wants? Where will that take me? To a place where I am no longer motivated by wants? To a place where I am no longer fearful? Is that a place I want to be? No, of course not. To utter such a prayer is crazy, is it not? Wouldn't any sane person go instead for the promise on the front page of the ad section, "Super savings on all your cravings"?

But note how the verse ends, "Shepherd me, O God, beyond my wants, beyond my fears, *from death into life.*" There is a kind of promise that's made, namely, that somewhere beyond my wants and fears there is a new kind of life, a life beyond the death in which I now find myself. Do I want that? Or have I now learned not to ask the "want" question anymore?

> The hymn verse is an exploration of the imagery found in Psalm 23:
> The Lord is my shepherd, I shall not want. . . .
> Though I walk through the valley of the shadow of death
> I fear no evil,
> For you are with me,
> Your rod and your staff they comfort me.

If that psalm makes the claim that neither death nor any other evil will befall those who walk with God, then it is surely false. If it makes the claim that those who walk with God will have all their wants fulfilled, it is false as well. But surely both the author and those in the congregation voicing this psalm knew that to be the case. Whatever else it was, the faith of these people was not a fairy tale. Yet, there is a very strong sense that for them life with God was a fulfilled human life: "You anoint my head with oil, my cup overflows. . . . And I will dwell in the house of the Lord forever."

Can we evaluate religions and faith commitments on how well and how completely they advance human fulfillment? I think we have, in the foregoing, seen several alternative answers:

- Yes, we can and ought to evaluate religions in exactly this way. Faith ought to serve human flourishing.

- No, we cannot, because the will of God or the life of faith is the only criterion that counts. It is the standard by which we measure human well-being. We do not measure the faith by how well it serves human well-being defined in some extra-faith sense.
- We should expect that faith will result in an altered view of ourselves and the world and an altered view of what is ultimately of value. But the new value is still, in the deepest sense, serving human well-being. So the answer here is either "Yes, but . . ." or "No, but . . ."
- This possibility may be just an alternative way of stating the previous one. It is to see the end of human well-being in constant and profound dialogue with the values embodied in the faith. Perhaps this is the point of making there be two "great commandments" (Matt. 22:38): "You shall love the Lord your God with all your heart and soul and mind . . . *and* you shall love your neighbor as yourself."

The first alternative fails because it could reduce everything to a question of prudence. The second fails because it can allow religion to become a kind of chauvinistic or self-sacrificial insanity. The third and fourth alternatives leave us in a dialogical uncertainty. But, to me at least, that is preferable to the juvenile clarity of the first option and the adolescent clarity of the second. I'm sorry I cannot get a better answer. Sometimes "yes, but . . ." and sometimes "no, but . . ." are as good as we can do.

Is Religious Faith Rational? One More Time Around

In the introduction, we talked briefly about the importance of beginning with the right question and the need to sometimes question the questions we begin with. (See p. 12.) There I stated:

> Many people . . . suppose that religious faith answers such questions as "What caused the universe? and "What happens to us after we die?" Such a beginning rests on the assumption that religion will answer for us questions that are at the edges, beyond our experience and our normal powers of knowing.
>
> I would suggest instead, echoing the twentieth-century Christian thinkers Dietrich Bonhoeffer and Thomas Merton, that religion answers questions that are at the very center—questions such as "What does it mean to be human?" and "How are we in the world?" and "How are

we with others?" The first set of questions sees God as transcendently high, transcendently long ago, or transcendently into the future. The second set sees God as transcendently deep and, odd as this may sound, transcendently present. The former questions are, I think, ones that can be avoided, or at least we can avoid answering them by simply saying that we do not know enough to answer them. The latter questions are ones that all humans answer in one way or another by the way we live our lives.

It is important to notice what happens when we shift from questions of the first sort to questions of the second sort. If we regard religious faith as answering questions of the first sort, then we are likely to see religious faith as the commitment to theoretical answers about the beginning of the cosmos or its end or other experience- and knowledge-transcending matters. If religion is seen as addressing such questions, it is easy to see why people assume that religion is a kind of theoretical belief rivaling or supplementing science. The question about whether such religion is rational then depends on the question of whether the theories are well evidenced and well argued—hence, arguments like the one between Collins and Dawkins we reviewed in the introduction.

If, on the other hand, we see religion as answering existential questions about the focus and orientation of human life, several things will be different: faith will be seen as more like life orientation and commitment than like theoretical belief, and the question about the rationality of faith will be about which way of envisioning the human produces the fullest, most completely human life. In other words, with a shift in the focal question, everything else changes, including the meaning of the question, "Is religious faith rational?"

Is religious faith a good thing? What can we learn from asking such a question? Certainly, we can't suppose that we will answer it in any kind of final way. A range of possible answers exists, from a clear "No, never" to a clear "Yes, always," with a large space in the middle for answers like "Maybe" or "It all depends."

Let's take a look at the reasons we might give for "yes" or "no" answers.

TABLE 1: IS RELIGION A GOOD THING?

NO	YES
Because religions try to answer questions that ought to be left to physics, biology, medicine, and economics	Because religion answers questions that other disciplines do not even raise—questions of hope, life orientation, and ultimate meaning
Because religious belief is a manifestation of juvenile helplessness continued into adulthood (Freud's argument)	Because faith empowers transformation of the self
Because religion perpetuates a juvenile punishment/reward ethics	Because religion takes us beyond a juvenile ethic and many other self-serving ethics
Because religion manifests chauvinistic us/them thinking and behavior and the violence that usually goes along with it	Because religion takes us beyond chauvinisms to seeing all humans as our brothers and sisters and as children of God
Because religion is a denial of reality, in particular, the reality of unjustified suffering and a chaotic universe, and it supplants active effort to change with a vain hope that justice will eventually be done (Marx's argument)	Because religion requires us to look suffering and injustice squarely in the face (argument of the Psalms, Job, and the Crucifixion narratives)
Because religion focuses on the poor and the suffering and the outcast and sees their characteristics (poverty, humility, pacifism, and obedience) as virtues (Nietzsche's argument)	Because religion focuses on the poor and the suffering and the outcast and sees their characteristics (poverty, humility, pacifism, and obedience as virtues).

This table raises several interesting points:

- In some cases, the very same thing is given as a reason for and a reason against religious faith.
- In many cases, a characteristic may be related to religion but it needn't be. Many religions are chauvinistic, but then so are many things that

are not religions (e.g., political and social movements and organizations). So, chauvinism is not characteristic of all religions, nor is it the case that all cases of chauvinism are religious.
- In several cases, religion is identified with a kind of juvenile view or behavior, and it is also identified as something that will empower us to move beyond such a juvenile view.
- In cases where genuine disagreement exists—for example, "Is religion violent or peaceful, juvenile or extremely mature?"—the answer is clearly "Yes, both." So what we notice is that religion is capable of being juvenile, chauvinistic, unrealistic, and violent, but it is also capable of being the very opposite. So, if we wish to draw a conclusion from this, we'd have to say, "It isn't religion that's problematic, but certain manifestations of it. It isn't religion in general that's wonderful and sublime, but only certain manifestations of it." In other words, we must avoid the wholesale judgment.

Can we then judge particular religions? We run into the same problem there. There is both chauvinistic and anti-chauvinistic Judaism, there is both violent and pacifist Islam, there is both juvenile and mature Christianity, and so forth.

Let us suppose, at this stage, that by "religious faith" here we mean a story-informed way of experiencing and being in the world. Is religious faith rational? The answer is, "That depends." But that is not a way of avoiding the question providing that we go on to explain what it depends upon. It depends on which religion one is talking about. Some religions promote chauvinism; some promote the siblinghood of all humans. Some promote inequality and violence; some promote a peaceful means to justice. Some promote a wasteful destruction of the planet; some promote earth stewardship. Some promote a cramped and diminished life; some promote a thriving humanity.

Religious questions are questions that cannot be avoided. We all answer them with the way we live our lives. Even total religious skeptics do that. They may not tell a religious story, but their life is informed by some story. Religious questions are questions about what the world is like, about how we are situated in it, about how we are related to other humans, about what we work at, attempt, dare, and hope. They are about how we attend to the world we live in and the life we have to live. Can these things be done in better and worse ways? I believe they can. Within the context of that "better and worse," the question of the rationality of faith has a legitimate and important place.

Some Concluding Thoughts

My contention throughout this book has been that belief is not, and never was, the heart of faith; that religious language is not, and never was, primarily referential; and that religious belief is not, and never was, evidentiary. Yet, we seem to have made and continue to make all of these mistakes.

I believe that philosophy of religion, developed as an argument about the evidences for the existence of God, has made a large contribution to this mistake. It has, in turn, influenced apologetics and other branches of theology, and these have influenced the thinking of the common culture. It would be interesting to trace the history of philosophy of religion to see when and where the rationality of theistic belief became the crucial issue in the intellectual discussion of faith.

Faith has tremendous power. It shapes people's lives; it even shapes entire cultures and civilizations, sometimes for good and sometimes for ill. Its power is far out of proportion to the evidences for the claim that God exists. Several thinkers have argued that the strength of faith ought to be proportional to the strength of the evidences for theistic belief. I believe we have shown that the strength of evidentiary arguments is quite irrelevant to the strength of faith. What is relevant is the strength of faith as a way of seeing, as a way of understanding the world, and as a way of more deeply understanding ourselves as humans in it.

When we encounter a religion, that is what we want to find out about it. We will not ask, "Are there Olympian gods on top of a mountain in Greece?" or its modern equivalent, but we should ask, "How do these stories and rites shape a view of the world and human beings?" We will not ask, "Did God create the world in six days?" But we should ask, "What is the view of the world and the human place in it that this story conveys?" We will not ask, "Were we really prisoners in Egypt liberated by a walk across the Red Sea?" But we may very well ask, "How do liberated slaves end up treating others?" We will not ask, "Was a baby born to a peasant couple in a census year in Bethlehem with a choir of angels, shepherds, and a parade of magi in attendance?" But we may ask, "What does 'God with us' look like? Emperor Augustus? Herod? The rich folks at the inn?" We will not ask, "Could Gautama Siddhartha really walk on water?" But we should ask, "What does the life of an awakened self look like?" We will not ask, "Is there a heavenly kingdom somewhere sometime?" But we should ask "What vision about our relation to our fellow humans does talk about 'the kingdom of God' communicate? What does living in the kingdom look like?"

Sometimes students complain that their studies in college have led to their "loss of faith." My guess is that what has actually occurred is the loss of beliefs that they supposed were the heart of faith. What I hope to have shown is that this is not the same thing as loss of faith at all, but simply an opportunity for a relocation or rediscovery of faith. Perhaps the student has then been liberated to ask the crucial questions: "What kind of world do I live in?" "How am I called to live as a human being within it?" "How do I understand my relation to others?" "How do I understand who I am?" All people will answer those questions by the way they live their lives. The possibility is that those lives will in turn be shaped by the ways of seeing embodied in the writings of the Bible, the Qur'an, the Gitas, and the teachings of Buddha, Jesus, and Mohammed.

I believe that the study of philosophy of religion should include a study of the theistic arguments but that it should not stop there. I believe it should go on to both notice and challenge the assumptions that traditional approach has made. We might thereby learn to see our own mistakes and avoid them, as well as be set on a more profitable line of inquiry.

Some Implications

The implications of refocusing what we understand to be the heart of faith, the nature of religious language, and the rationality of faith are no doubt beyond my imagining. Yet, just a few things occur to me here. Refocusing faith and the understanding of religious discourse in the ways suggested in this book could result in the following:

- A refocusing of attention not primarily on the putative subjects of our informing stories but on the ways of experiencing and on the lives that are informed by them. The focal question would then be "How do you live?" rather than "By what name are you called?" The consequence would be to notice similarities among faith communities as well as great differences within them.

- Seeing religious eclecticism and religious pluralism as a real possibility. Mohandas Gandhi saw this and practiced it, claiming for himself essential elements from all of the world's great religions. Thomas Merton, Christian monk, practiced a dialogue of Christianity and Buddhism and maintained that his appreciation of each was enhanced by his study and practice of the other.
- The avoidance of religious chauvinism on the grounds that "since my faith is right, yours must be wrong." Not all religiously inspired ways of seeing are compatible. Some clearly rule out others. But my perception is that several may be more than compatible. They may be complementary and even congruent.
- Religious creativity. There is no reason to suppose that the last informing story has been written or the last great myth has been acted out or sung. Why can't there be such a thing as religious creativity? Is devotion to some ancient form the only shape a legitimate faith can take?
- An avoidance of all sorts of intractable theological problems that occur only if we take theological discourse to be primarily referential rather than primarily life informing. Though the struggle with evil should be central to any faith community, the "problem of evil" as traditionally defined will largely disappear. It depends too much on the assumptions of the focality of belief, the referential character of God-language, the existence of God as a person-like agent, and so forth. When those assumptions are no longer made, the problem will not be solved, but I believe it will dissipate. In its place, we can focus attention on how we respond to human suffering and world destruction, on what meaning we give to human solidarity and hope.
- Along with the rethinking of theological problems will come a rethinking of the meaning of theology. An example is provided in this quote by Nicholas Lash: "And this unceasing, strenuous, vulnerable attempt to make some Christian sense of things, not just in what we say, but through the ways in which we 'see' the world is what is known as theology." [4]
- Theology, rather than being an effort to talk about God, may evolve into God-informed ways of talking about the world. The heart of theology will be, then, its ethics, its sociology, its economics, and so forth.

- A relocation of religion and religious study, not set off as some separate field of expertise but as deeply embedded in the whole multidimensional business of being human in the world. I am reminded of titles like "Buddhist Economics," "Biblical Environmentalism," "Christian Twelve Step Programs: Their Psychology and Sociology," and "The Nation State: A Muslim Critique." Rather than seeing such studies as being tangential expressions of a faith community, we might come to see them as absolutely central.

FROM THE CLASSROOM: STUDENT QUESTIONS & RESPONSES

Q: You claim that Newton's paradigm is analogous to the God paradigm. However, we can observe Newton's laws working in everyday life, but we don't see God acting in the world. Newtonian science is verifiable in a way that God-talk is not. So it seems that the analogy doesn't work.

R: Well, I don't agree. A person who sees the world as God's gift or who sees his neighbor as a child of God sees God at work everywhere, just like a Newtonian sees gravity at work everywhere. The psalmist writes: "The heaven and earth are full of Thy handiwork" (Ps. 104). I think they're very analogous. You're making an interesting assumption that you'd do well to uncover if you think you can see gravity at work but you can't see God.

Q: Your approach seems to imply that the referential part of religion is mistaken. If one carried through on that, wouldn't religion just turn into a kind of ethics? Maybe that's what it should become? In ethics, one is not expected to believe anything, just to live a particular kind of life. It's often the belief part of a religion that's chauvinistic. A lot of religions agree on their ethics.

R: That's a very provocative question. But ethics itself isn't just a list of rules for life. Our actions are shaped by how we understand ourselves, others, and the world. These things are shaped, in turn, by what I might call "informing metaphors." If I look at myself and others as inhabiting a competitive video game sort of world where you have to devour others before they devour you, then a certain pattern of action will follow. If I see the world as divided up between "us" and "them," then a certain pattern of behavior results. On the other hand, if I see myself and others as brothers and sisters or, as Gandhi put it, "all children of one God," then a very different life pattern emerges. My point is that ethics are more like religions than we might suppose.

Q: I found the example of your paranoid student to be fascinating. But what's your point? Is it that religions may be internally coherent and rational but externally irrational and false? If so, what's the point of talking to such people?

R: I use the word *false* to talk about the student's delusion, but the problem was that there was no way to demonstrate its falseness. I couldn't say to him, "Here's your world and here's the real world; see how different they are?" The "falsehood" of his world had to become apparent *to him*. It did so as the influence of the drugs wore off and as he came to see that his view no longer worked for him.

The point of the example is simply to show how difficult a discussion about the rationality of an informing vision or assumption can be. How could I convince a religious zealot that his plan to kill all the infidels is insane? Won't he see all my arguments and appeals to rationality as evidence of my infidelity? The only thing I could do is what I did for my student: model for him the care and rationality I would have him come back to.

Q: You seem to be saying that some faiths are rationally vindicated and some are not. Of those that are not, are we justified in judging them irrational, perhaps even making the practice of them illegal?

R: It may seem awfully judgmental, but it seems to me we do that already. We praise freedom of religion as one of the founding principles of our democracy. But, in practice, that freedom is pretty limited. We do not allow the practice of human sacrifice, for example. When the treaties were written that ended the war with Japan, we allowed some elements of Shinto religion to remain (for example, the reverence for the Japanese emperor) while severely restricting others (for example, the cult of the Kamikaze). The religion of Puritan Protestants remains, but the witch trials they practiced have been made illegal. The Roman Catholic Church remains, but the inquisitions that were practiced in Spain and Italy would now probably be counted as "crimes against humanity." Religious practice should definitely not be beyond criticism or beyond limitation.

Q: What do you call your approach to philosophy of religion? Does it fit into a particular philosophical category?

R: Since I borrow unashamedly from so many sources, I suppose it should be called an eclectic approach. But, more particularly, I would say it is critical and analytic in part, pragmatic in part, but also phenomenological, analogical, and imaginatively constructive. I don't think there's a particular name for such a combination.

QUESTIONS FOR CRITICAL REFLECTION

1. "Newton's discovery of gravity was not discovering a new reality but finding a new way to look at all of reality." Do you agree with that assessment of Newton? Can you find other exemplars in the history of science to whom it applies?

2. "Jesus' discovery of the kingdom of God was not discovering a new reality but finding a new way to look at all of reality." Do you agree? Do you object to the parallel with Newton?

3. Evaluate the suggestion that God functions as a paradigm shaping our attention rather than as an object of attention.

4. "It is a great waste of time to try to verify (or falsify) faith claims." Do you agree? Disagree? If you agree, is it for the same reasons given in this text?

5. How should philosophy of religion as a discipline change? How should an undergraduate course in this area be taught? How should it not be taught?

6. How would you answer the question "Is religious faith rational?" As the author has? Explain your reasons for your agreement or disagreement with his answer.

7. Are there other important implications of refocusing faith than those enumerated at the end of this section?

GLOSSARY

agape, agapeistic: Christianity—one of the Greek words for "love." The kind of sacrificial love Christ embodied.

agnostic: One who believes there is insufficient evidence to settle the question whether God does or does not exist.

atheist: One who believes that God does not exist.

baptism: Christianity—the sacramental washing of a person upon joining or becoming welcomed into the worshipping community.

bodhisattva: Buddhism—a person who has achieved nirvana but who has, out of compassion, returned to help those who still dwell in illusion.

Buddha: Literally, one who has awakened or been enlightened. Secondarily, Gautama Siddhartha, Indian teacher revered by Buddhists.

cosmological argument: An argument for the existence of God that begins with a premise describing some feature of the cosmos, such as causality.

deconstruct, deconstructionism: To explicate and critique the assumptions on which a way of thinking or acting is based. A twentieth-century philosophical movement focused on explicating and challenging the assumptions of modernism.

dharma: Buddhism—the essential teachings of the Buddha

epistemic, epistemology: Making a knowledge claim. The theory of knowledge.

Eucharist: Christianity—the sacred meal in which bread and wine are presented as the body and blood of Christ.

free-will defense: A theodicy that attempts to explain moral evil by seeing it as a consequence of God's respect for human free will.

glossary: A list of technical or unfamiliar words and their meanings.

henotheism: The belief that though there are many gods, one of them is the chief or ruling divinity. Example: Zeus as "Lord and father of all" and ruler of other gods in the Olympic pantheon.

heresy, heretic: A belief that is not orthodox. A person whose belief has been condemned by the religious authorities.

heterodox, heterodoxy: Literally, "different belief." Not in alignment with usual belief or interpretation. Believing something different from the orthodox.

incarnation: Literally, "in the flesh." The Christian belief that the person, Jesus, was God incarnate.

immanence, immanent: Something of great religious significance that is present in the ordinary world. Contrast to transcendence.

ineffable: Something that is so unique it cannot be expressed in language.

intentional activity: Any activity that can be willed or undertaken deliberately and purposively.

jihad: Islam—a struggle. Secondarily, a holy war.

karma: Hinduism—the belief that actions performed in a previous life affect one's caste or welfare in this (or some future) life.

logo-centric: A way of thinking that is heavily word-focused.

metaphysics, metaphysical: The philosophical study of the basic structure of reality. Sometimes used to designate a realm of reality beyond the physical.

monotheism: The theistic belief in the unity or singularity of God. Contrast polytheism, henotheism.

moral evil: The evil that is in the world due to human choice and action (for example, torture, war, rape, and so on.) Contrast to natural evil.

naturalism: The view that the natural sciences provide a vocabulary rich enough to describe all of reality.

natural evil: Evil that is in the world due to natural disasters (for example, plagues and tsunamis).

non-referential language: Language that gets its meaning by some other means than by referring to things in the world. Examples include performative language or functional language.

non-theistic religions: Religions that do not have a belief in God or gods or in which such belief plays a minor role.

ontological argument: A theistic argument based on the inference that the existence of God is demonstrated from an understanding of God's essence or nature.

orthodox, orthodoxy: Literally, right belief. Those beliefs identified by religious authority as necessary and correct. Contrast to heterodox, heterodoxy, and heresy.

pantheon: Literally, all gods. All the gods of a polytheistic tradition.

paradigm: A model or best example.

paradigm shift: The change in point of view that occurs from adopting a new model.

performative language: Language that does not describe a situation, but performs an action. Example: "I now pronounce you husband and wife."

polytheist: The theistic belief in many gods. Contrast to monotheist.

pragmatic, pragmatist: Derived from the Greek root meaning "practice," an act is pragmatic if it meets some practical need. A pragmatist is a philosopher who believes that an idea or theory should be tested by how it works in practice.

reductionism: The intellectual temptation (fallacy) to reduce a complex reality to one of its parts or dimensions.

referential language: Language that derives its meaning from naming or describing some thing or state of affairs in the world. Contrast to non-referential language.

Sangha: Buddhism—the Buddhist religious community. The community of bikhus, mendicant monks.

sound argument: A deductive argument that is both valid and has a complete set of true premises.

supernatural, supernaturalism: The view that there is a domain of reality beyond the natural world.

Tanakh: Judaism—the Hebrew Bible consisting of the five books of Moses, the prophets, and other writings.

theistic argument: An argument for or against the existence of God.

theism: The belief in a god or gods. Contrast to atheism and agnosticism.

theodicy: A philosophical argument meant to explain how a good God could have created an apparently evil world.

transcendence, transcendent: That which lies beyond. The world beyond the ordinary world of life and experience. Examples include heaven and the afterlife.

ultimate: The last item in an ascending scale of comparison. Examples: the highest number, the most perfect being, the best performance.

ultimate concern: A phrase theologian Paul Tillich used to talk about the reality of God. The final end, that by which everything else in life is to be evaluated.

valid argument: A deductive argument in which, if the premises are true, the conclusion must be true.

world religion: Any religion that is practiced by persons in all the inhabited continents of the world.

WORKS CITED

Anselm of Canterbury. *St. Anselm: Basic Writings*. Translated by S. N. Deane. La Salle, Ill.: Open Court, 1962.

Aquinas, Thomas. *Summa Theologica: Basic Writings of Thomas Aquinas*. Edited by Anton C. Pegis. New York: Random House, 1965.

Armstrong, Karen. *The Case for God*. New York: Knopf, 2009.

Batchelor, Stephen. *Buddhism without Beliefs: A Contemporary Guide to Awakening*. New York: Riverhead, 1997.

Berry, Wendell. "Manifesto: The Mad Farmer Liberation Front." In *The Country of Marriage*. New York: Harcourt Brace, Jovanovich, 1973.

Bonhoeffer, Dietrich. *Letters and Papers from Prison*. New York: Simon & Schuster, 1997.

Borg, Marcus. *The Heart of Christianity: Rediscovering a Life of Faith*. San Francisco: Harper Collins, 2003.

Bouwsma, O. K. "The Mystery of Time." In *Philosophical Essays*. Lincoln: University of Nebraska Press, 1965.

Braithwaite, Richard. "An Empiricist's View of the Nature of Religious Belief." In *The Philosophy of Religion: Oxford Readings in Philosophy*, edited by Basil Mitchell. London: Oxford University Press, 1971.

Buber, Martin. *I and You*. Edited and translated by Tom Christenson. Unpublished edition. Original *Ich und Du*, published 1923.

Carroll, Lewis. "Alice through the Looking Glass." In *The Complete Illustrated Works of Lewis Carroll*. London: Chancellor, 1982.

Carse, James P. *The Religious Case against Belief.* New York: Penguin, 2008.

Clayton, Phillip. *Transforming Christian Theology for Church and Society*. Minneapolis: Augsburg Fortress, 2008.

Crombie, I. M. "The Possibility of Theological Statements." In *Faith and Logic*, edited by Basil Mitchell. London: George Allen & Unwin, 1957.

Crosson, John Dominic. *The Dark Interval: The Theology of Story*. Chicago: Eagle, Poleridge, 1975.

Descartes, Rene. *Meditations on First Philosophy.* Translated by Laurence Lafleur. New York: Macmillan/Library of Liberal Arts, 1960.

Dykstra, Craig. *Vision & Character: A Christian Educators Alternative to Kohlberg*. New York: Paulist, 1981.

Evans, C. Stephen. *Why Believe? Reason and Mystery as Pointers to God*. Grand Rapids: Eerdmans, 1996.

Farrar, Austin. "A Starting Point for the Philosophical Examination of Theological Belief." In *Faith and Logic*, edited by Basil Mitchell. London: George Allen & Unwin, 1957.

Ferré, Frederick. "The Definition of Religion." *Journal of the American Academy of Religion* 38, no. 1 (1970): 3–16.

Fiddler on the Roof. Lyrics by Sheldon Harnish and music by Jerry Bok (1964).

Freud, Sigmund. *The Future of an Illusion*. Translated by W. D. Robson-Scott. Garden City, N.Y.: Anchor/Doubleday, 1964.

Frye, Northrup. *The Educated Imagination*. Toronto: Anansi House, 2002.

Green, Garrett. *Imagining God: Theology and the Religious Imagination*. Grand Rapids: Eerdmans, 1989.

Hesiod. *Theogony.* Translated by Norman O. Brown. Indianapolis: Library of Liberal Arts, 1964.

Hick, John. "Religious Faith as Experiencing-As." In *Talk of God*. London: Macmillan/St. Martin's, 1969.

Holy Bible: Revised Standard Version. New York: Thomas Nelson & Sons, 1959.

Hume, David. *Dialogues Concerning Natural Religion*. New York: Hafner, 1948.

James, William. "Pragmatism: A New Name for Some Old Ways of Thinking." In *Pragmatism and Other Writings*. New York: Penguin Classics, 2000.

———. *The Will to Believe and Other Essays*. New York: Library of America, 1992.

Jones, W. T. *The Classical Mind: The History of Western Philosophy*. New York: Harcourt Brace Jovanovich, 1969.

Kant, Immanuel. *Critique of Pure Reason*. Translated by Norman Kemp Smith. London: Macmillan, 1963.

Kaufman, Gordon D. *God the Problem*. Cambridge, Mass.: Harvard University Press, 1972.

Kierkegaard, Søren. *The Concluding Unscientific Postscript*. Princeton: Translated by Howard and Edna Hong. Princeton: Princeton University Press, 1964.

Kushner, Harold. *Who Needs God?* New York: Simon & Schuster, 1989.

Lao Tzu. *Tao Te Ching*. Translated by Gia-Fu Feng and Jane English. New York: Vintage/Random House, 1972.

Lash, Nicholas. *Holiness, Speech and Silence: Reflections on the Question of God*. Cambridge: Cambridge University Press, 2004.

Luther, Martin. *The Small Catechism*. Minneapolis: Augsburg Fortress, 1988.

Marion, Jean Luc. *God without Being*. Chicago: University of Chicago Press, 1991.

Karl Marx. "Critique of Hegel's Philosophy of Right." In *Selected Writings*, edited by David McLellan. Oxford: Oxford University Press, 1977.

Marx, Karl, and Friedrich Engels. *On Religion*. New York: Schocken, 1964.

Merton, Thomas. *Choosing to Love the World*. Boulder: Sounds True, 2008.

Niebuhr, H. Richard. *The Responsible Self: An Essay in Christian Moral Philosophy*. New York: Harper & Row, 1963.

Nietzsche, Friedrich. *Beyond Good & Evil*. Translated by R.J. Hollingdale. New York: Penguin, 1999.

Nhat Hanh, Thich. *Old Path, White Clouds: Walking in the Footsteps of the Buddha*. Berkeley: Parallax, 1991.

Norris, Kathleen. *Amazing Grace: A Vocabulary of Faith*. New York: Riverhead, 1998.

———. *Dakota: A Spiritual Geography.* New York: Ticknor & Fields, 1993.

Paley, William. *Natural Theology.* Indianapolis: Library of Liberal Arts, 1945.

Phillips, D. Z. *The Concept of Prayer.* London: Routledge, Kegan Paul, 1965.

———. *Faith and Philosophical Enquiry.* London: Routledge, Kegan Paul, 1970.

Pojman, Louis P. *Philosophy of Religion.* Mountain View, Calif.: Mayfield, 2001.

The Qur'an. Translated by Abdullah Yosif Ali. Elmhurst, N.Y.: Tarike Tarsile Qur'an, 2001.

Rahner, Karl. "Poetry and the Christian." In Theological *Investigations*, translated by David Morland. New York: Seabury, 1979.

Smith, Wilfred Cantwell. *Faith and Belief.* Princeton, N.J.: Princeton University Press, 1979.

Swift, Jonathan. *Gulliver's Travels.* Oxford: Oxford University Press, 2005.

This I Believe: The Personal Philosophies of Remarkable Men and Women. Edited by Jay Allison & Don Gedwinn. New York: Henry Holt & Co., 2007.

Tillich, Paul. *The Dynamics of Faith.* New York: Harper & Row, 1957.

———. *The Theology of Culture.* New York: Oxford University Press, 1959.

Westphal, Merold. *Overcoming Onto-theology: Toward a Postmodern Christian Faith.* New York: Fordham University Press, 2001.

———. *Suspicion and Faith: The Religious Uses of Modern Atheism.* Grand Rapids: Eerdmans, 1993.

Whitehead, Alfred North. *Religion in the Making.* New York: Meridian, 1960.

Zlotkowski, Theodore. *Modes of Faith: Secular Surrogates for Lost Religious Belief.* Chicago: University of Chicago Press, 2007.

ANNOTATED SUGGESTIONS FOR FURTHER READING

Students interested in reading further into the topics discussed here might consider the following works and authors who represent widely varying points of view:

Barbour, Ian G. *Myths, Models, and Paradigms: A Comparative Study in Science and Religion*. New York: Harper & Row, 1974.
    A comparison of the use of language in religion and science and the use of myths, models, and paradigms in both.

Frederick Ferré, Joseph J. Kocklemans, and John E. Smith, eds. *The Challenge of Religion: Contemporary Readings in Philosophy of Religion*. New York: Seabury, 1982.
    A very good anthology of essays on contemporary philosophy of religion.

Green, Garrett. *Imagining God: Theology and the Religious Imagination*. Grand Rapids: Eerdmans, 1989.
    A positive review of the uses of poetic imagination in the process of theological thinking and a warning against what happens when we no longer notice the metaphorical character of our language.

James, William. "The Will to Believe." In *The Will to Believe and Other Essays in Popular Philosophy*. New York: Library of America, 1992.

James's classic essay challenges the conclusion that belief is not something that can be intentionally chosen. Hence, he talks about the *will* to believe. It is interesting to note the examples of belief he uses to make his argument as well as the role he sees faith playing in people's lives.

Kaufman, Gordon D. *God the Problem*. Cambridge, Mass.: Harvard University Press, 1972.

Kaufman, for many decades professor of theology at Harvard, explores in this book why God is a problem for many moderns. He addresses how talk about God is related to science and has a particularly useful discussion of God and the problem of evil.

Phillips, D. Z. *Faith and Philosophical Inquiry*. London: Routledge, Kegan Paul, 1970.

Phillips, D. Z. *The Concept of Prayer*. London: Routledge, Kegan Paul, 1965.

In these and other of his writings, Phillips, an interpreter of the work of Ludwig Wittgenstein and Soren Kierkegaard, among others, looks at the role that faith plays in people's lives and the kind of absolute commitment it seems to require. In the book on prayer, he examines the questions "What is it we do when we pray?" and "What kinds of transformations does prayer occasion?"

Plantinga, Alvin. *Warranted Christian Belief*. New York: Oxford University Press, 2000.

This is a very thorough defense of the rationality of Christian belief not through the presentation of evidential arguments but through a defense of the view that Christian belief in God is properly basic—that is, it needs no evidential arguments in order to be a warranted belief. But the book also features several discussions that would particularly interest someone reading this monograph: for example, Plantinga's criticism of the views of Gordon Kaufman and John Hick or his criticism of the consistency of Christianity with Kantian, post-Kantian and post-modern views.

Weiss, Paul. *Modes of Being.* Carbondale, Ill.: Southern Illinois University Press, 1958.

Weiss argues that existence is one of four "modes of being" and that God is another and separate mode. Not an easy book by any means, it raises a host of important questions for the philosophy of religion.

Westphal, Merold. *Overcoming Onto-Theology: Toward a Post-Modern Christian Faith.* New York: Fordham University Press, 2001.

Westphal responds to Plantinga's arguments and argues for the possibility of a postmodern Christian view. He does an admirable job of trying to explain Martin Heidegger's criticism of onto-theology, the view that God is to be thought of primarily as a kind of being and that religious language is to be understood mainly as referential.

Westphal, Merold. *Suspicion and Faith: The Religious Uses of Modern Atheism.* Grand Rapids: Eerdmans, 1993.

Westphal expertly summarizes the religious criticisms of Freud, Nietzsche, and Marx. But rather than trying to refute their criticism, he takes it as largely justified and asks instead, "What can Christians learn from this?"

Whitehead, Alfred North. *Religion in the Making.* New York: Meridian, 1960.

This is not an easy book to read. Whitehead talks about religion and God in the context of his philosophical worldview usually referred to as "process philosophy." In some parts it's hard to get a handle on Whitehead's language, but in other parts his comments are extremely novel and provocative. Reading this short book will be a significant learning experience for the student willing to be challenged.

INDEX

"all men are created equal," 34, 79–80, 98
Anselm of Canterbury, 2
Aquinas, Thomas, 2
Aristotle, 8, 46
Armstrong, Karen, 11, 14–15
Augustine of Hippo, 49

Barbour, Ian, 135
belief
    belief-in and belief-that, 33
    epistemic and pragmatic, 35
    etymology of the term, 37–38
    not univocal, 32
Berry, Wendell, 90–92
Bonhoeffer, Dietrich, 12, 123
Bouwsma, O. K., 50, 52
Buber, Martin, 82

Carroll, Lewis, 25, 48–49
Carse, James P., 20–22
Christmas poem 2007, 68–69
Collins–Dawkins debate, 5–7

Crombie, I. M., 85 ff.
Crossan, John Dominic, 73

Darwin, Charles, 3
Descartes, Rene, 2
Doctor Suess, 93
"Do You Love Me?", 48–49
Dykstra, Craig, 81

Evans, C. Stephen, 11
experiencing-as, 84, 109, 123

faith
    defined, 76
    loss of, 122
    rationality of, 110, 113, 117, 118
Ferre, Frederick, 28
freedom of religion, 125
Freud, Sigmund, 104–5
Frye, Northrup, 73

Gandhi, Mohandas K., 123
God-language, how it is used, 59–61

God, paradigm, 126
gravity, 78–79, 96–97
Green, Garrett, 135

Hick, John, 84–85
Horse's Mouth, The, 71, 72
Hume, David, 3

James, William, 36, 100–101, 136
Jefferson Thomas, 79–80
Jones, W. T., 50

Kant, Immanuel, 2
Kaufman, Gordon, 136
Kierkegaard, Søren, 22
Kushner, Harold, 67

Lash, Nicholas, 9
Leibniz, Gottfried, 4

Marx, Karl, 103
meliorism, 101
Merton, Thomas, 12
myth, defined, 107

Newton, Isaac, 78–79, 96–97
Niebuhr, H. Richard, 81
Nietzsche, Friedrich, 101–3
Nhat Hanh, Thich, 70–71
Norris, Kathleen, 21–22

Paley, William, 2–3
parable, 73 ff.

paranoid student story, 111–12, 125
Phillips. D. Z., 136
Plantinga, Alvin, 4
Pojman, Louis, 28
pragmatism, 100 ff.

Rahner, Karl, 74–75
referentialist assumption, 57
religion
    defined, 107
    a good thing?, 119, 120
    as a way of seeing, 67
religious discourse, a theory, 89–90
resurrection, the practice of, 90–92

Shinto, 125
Smith, Wilfred Cantwell, 37
Swift, Jonathan, 55

Table 1: "Is Religion a Good Thing?", 119
Taoism, 20
theistic arguments, 1 ff.
theology, redefined, 123
Tillich, Paul, 27

Warnock, Mary, 81
Weiss, Paul, 137
Westphal, Merold, 106, 137
Whitehead, A. N., 137

Yankton Dakota community, 20